GOOGLE ADS and SEO

Learn All About Google and SEO and How to Use Their Powers for Your Business (2022 Guide for Beginners)

Mark Marshman

1

TABLE OF CONTENTS

INTRODUCTION

Googling is a phrase that literally means "search with Google, do a search over the telematic network, and have been utilizing the Google search engine since 2008." This is because Google is the most popular search engine in the world, and we all use it to conduct preliminary research before making a purchase, booking a trip, or using a service, knowing that the first results that surface will be the best and most relevant.

In fact, the Google algorithm is subject to continuous updates in order to be able to evaluate the various contents in the best possible way, preventing the "smarties" from taking the first places and thus ensuring their own authority in the classification of results based on the quality of the site and the information contained therein.

Appearing first, on the first page of Google results, allows you to be found at the precise moment the user is seeking for us, boosting the probability of a sale and making your business known. But how can you get to the first page of Google?

The ability to market a product or service to a highly profiled customer who is searching for exactly what you wish to promote is a significant advantage of Google placement. Unlike traditional advertising methods (web banners, flyers, radio or television promotions), which focus on invasive communication by showing our promotions to users who are not looking for them, natural positioning on search engines is aimed at interested users, responding to the search for potential customers who are looking for our product and will thus have the opportunity to access our services.

To get increased exposure in organic searches and a good Google ranking, it is important to be aligned with the criteria of its algorithm, implementing a series of technicalities and techniques contained in SEO, "Search Engine Optimization," or search engine optimization. To do it well, of course, you need a lot of experience and in-depth understanding of Google: you can't improvise on results. It is critical to rely on a knowledgeable SEO expert who can optimize the contents already present on the site or generate new ones in order to place it higher and higher on search engines, increasing visibility and, consequently, visits.

Once the decision to appear with your firm on the web has been made, the next step is to define the method, cost, and strategy of this presence, as well as to outline the objectives and expected results. But first, let's define the distinction between SEO and Ads campaigns.

SEO is used to optimize a website in order to rank higher in search results, whereas SEM goes a step further. Other tactics that can attract more visitors, such as PPC advertising, are used in the latter procedure.

Both alternatives are essential for a web marketing campaign: one does not preclude the other, and it is best to combine them to cover all of the market's niches and potential.

Ads concentrate on the present in order to attain short-term objectives.

SEM is a marketing method that aims to improve search engine exposure by getting "free" traffic through SEO or paid traffic through paid advertising.

The most well-known advertising option is Google Adverts, which allows you to have ads display in a specific section of Google search results and pay solely for clicks on your ads.

You then purchase advertising space in search engine results, rather than attempting to rank higher and gain organic traffic (which is possible with SEO), you pay to appear at the top of the search engine SERPs.

This is also why the technique is known as Pay-per-click, or PPC. Although Bing and Yahoo have similar systems, they have never been as effective as Google Ads.

Because it is targeted, SEM traffic is regarded as the most important source of web traffic. People today use search engines to locate a solution to a problem, an answer to a query, or to learn how to do something.

As a result, when users "land" on a website from search results or by clicking on an ad, their odds of conversion increase significantly. SEM traffic is more useful than any other source due to the relevance of the sites and advertisements presented.

Is it enough to have a website, a budget, and an advertisement to be competitive on the internet?

It's not that easy; PPC advertising must also be optimized! As a sponsored positioning, it is critical that it works, both on the user and algorithm sides.

The common denominator is the consistency of each campaign element: the more the consistency across search queries, ad, extensions, and landing page, the higher the quality score provided by Google and the better the user reaction. It is critical to make the ad and landing page appealing to the user while also adhering to the algorithm's rules.

You must also maintain focus on the campaign's aim and the strategy you choose to implement. There are automatic techniques for managing the investment budget, in which Google decides how much to offer per click, and manual CPC strategies, in which the campaign manager actively changes the maximum CPC.

Long-term investment in SEO

SEO is the process of optimizing a website in order to increase organic traffic from search engines. An optimized website is easier for search engine crawlers to understand, increasing the odds of ranking the site as high as possible in the SERP.

The organic results are the results offered by Google in response to each Query that are deemed to be the best in terms of competency and quality of information pertaining to the user's search.

Today, these results are more adaptable: SERPs alter according on the user's interests, location, device, time, day of the week, and type of search, among other things.

To achieve good results, a number of procedures performed by the SEO Specialist are required prior to delivering a hierarchically structured site in code and content that will be appreciated by Google bots and users.

The outcomes of the operations in this area are not immediate. The age of the content is also a factor in organic ranking, thus it may take some time for a page to reach the top places.

As the ascent is sluggish, so is the drop; in fact, the positions attained remain more or less steady, with possible variations, ensuring long-term outcomes spanning months and years.

After examining the competition and the market, the SEO expert will begin with the optimization of your website and content.

The results acquired via effort and determination to reach Google's good graces are prolonged throughout time, determining a significant distinction between SEO and Ads.

The quality of the content is an important factor in SEO since the Google algorithm determines how beneficial a website is in terms of utility or User Experience for the user who conducts the search.

Another important factor that Google considers is the presence of links to your site from other websites.

The more prominent the site holding a link pointing to you, the more authoritative Google will consider you to be.

SEO and Google Ads are not mutually exclusive!

As previously said, naturally placing yourself on search engines takes time.

We can't rely on SEO if we have a product to debut, an impending event to advertise, or if we need to become public with our new firm right away to build authority.

The choice between SEO and Google Ads campaigns is not exclusive, as both investments have advantages, and by combining the two types of web marketing into a single strategy, the results can be maximized.

A competent and well-structured Web Agency can advise businesses on how to allocate their budget between the two expenditures, maximizing the potential of SEO and PPC campaigns:

The web presence can be developed instantly, and it hopes to grow naturally using SEO in the meanwhile.

You can use Ads to cover keywords for which you are not organically positioned.

When the same website shows in both paid and organic results for a specific keyword at the same time, the statistics demonstrate how you increase your click-through / impression rate over individual results. Increasing a brand's presence in a

SERP using all accessible tactics promotes customer trust in the brand.

So, how should you decide between SEO and Google Ads campaigns?

You should now understand what SEO is and how it varies from advertising. You've probably realized that SEO is an essential component of any web marketing strategy.

SEO should never be disregarded because it is the only way to ensure your professional websites' long-term success.

Purchasing traffic with Google Ads or Pay-Per-Click is an excellent technique to maximize the impact of your marketing strategy.

It will provide immediate traffic to your website, and if the campaign is properly put up, it will provide your organization with a method to stand out from the crowd, or to promote a new product or an upcoming event.

The techniques to be implemented vary depending on the goals to be attained. Because the materials must be of high quality and the result of rigorous investigation, you will nearly always require the assistance of professionals.

CHAPTER 1

SEO TOOLS: THESE ARE THE BEST TOOLS FOR EASY SEO

If you're new to the wonderful world of Search Engine Optimization, you're probably wondering which SEO tool to use to index your material.

Search engine optimization is a fundamental activity not only in digital marketing but in the entire process of creating an online business. If you want your clients to find you when they Google something related to your business or eCommerce, you'll need to excel at SEO and Content Marketing. There is a lot of competition out there!

The good news is that SEO is simple: the laws of Search Engine Optimization are numerous, but they are also simple to understand and easily accessible online.

Instead, how about the awful one? It is a complex, time-consuming endeavor that necessitates a healthy dose of ingenuity and the capacity to analyze data.

As a result, there are innumerable SEO tools available online that may (and should) be used to make our lives easier and to do a better job. There are so many, though, that selecting the correct tool for our requirements can be the most difficult of all!

What are the functions of SEO tools?

As previously said, there are hundreds, if not thousands, of SEO tools available online. But why are there so many of them? Are they all the same?

Obviously not; on the contrary, the reason for the creation of this jungle is that SEO is a complex activity that entails a number of activities.

There is SEO research, which is the search for keywords for which to index content.

Then there's on-site SEO, which comprises all of the activities that may be done within the site to get noticed by search engines. This contains both items to be used in the development of content and code to be put into the page structure (structured data, schema, meta tags, etc).

Finally, there is off-site SEO, which covers all of the

external factors to keep an eye on, such as links from other sites, social activities, and so on.

Each of these macro-areas is made up of numerous passageways and contains a variety of materials. There is a Search Engine Optimization tool that is specifically designed for each. Obviously, at vastly different costs!

Are you beginning to see why it's so complicated?

Don't worry, we're here to assist you to figure out which SEO tools are best for you by categorizing them (with an eye to the price).

So let's start at the beginning, with the first task to perform when approaching SEO: keyword research.

Keyword research software

Keyword research, or keyword research, is one of the most exciting and delicate jobs to undertake because the success of the entire website is dependent on its success.

The goal of this analysis is to find the right keywords, i.e. the keywords that:

Have a high enough monthly search volume to generate traffic

Do not have excessive competition from content positioned for the same keyword in the google serp

Are related to the products or services you offer

Are specific enough to carry qualified traffic, and so on.

14

In short, the proper keywords cannot be invented but must be investigated, evaluated, and analyzed using SEO Tools notes.

Google's own keyword research tools are the first to consider (especially because they are the greatest free SEO tools).

Google's free SEO keyword research tools

Given that Google is by far the most popular search engine in the world, it stands to reason that the first SEO analyses are conducted using its tools.

They are unquestionably accurate (the data source is the same) and are freely available. The issue is that several distinct stages are required to provide a thorough analysis, and they are frequently difficult to utilize, making everything extremely time-consuming (which is why there are so many other much more expensive SEO tools).

Google Keyword Planner is a good place to start.

To use this tool (which is primarily used for SEM or the purchase of advertising space), you must first create a Google Ads account, and once registered, you will have access to a wealth of information provided directly by Google.

Starting with a keyword, you can observe search trends (a tool recently added by Google Trends), volume, an estimate of competitiveness, and Ad purchase costs. Furthermore, Google suggests "related terms," or other keywords that may be appropriate to use in conjunction with the main keyword, in the upper section.

To get other keyword ideas, as well as an idea of the competition and how the topics are addressed by competitors, simply do a search on Google (using Incognito Mode so that the results are not distorted by our history): with the automatic completion, we will get many other alternative ideas to aim for, and for each, we will be able to open the first results obtained to verify the contents, etc.

Isn't it simple? However, as previously stated, it takes a significant amount of time.

Other valuable SEO tools that supplement and combine the information provided by Google can be used for this purpose.

Answer The General Public's Response The Public is a free tool (at least in its basic functions) that does nothing more than taking everything that is searched on Google in relation to a specific term, but also on forums and social media, and propose it again in the form of "aggregate data" depending on numerous parameters, such as:

Questions (how, when, why, etc)

Prepositions (with, on, for, etc)

Comparisons (vs, against, o, etc)

And in alphabetical order

As a result, this instrument provides a rich mine of ideas for articles, thoughts, materials, and so on. One of the first places to start for any self-respecting SEO researcher.

People Also Ask is a similar application that simply presents user searches in the form of questions.

The issue is that neither of them gives quantifiable data such as the number of monthly searches, the difficulty of ranking, and so on. To obtain them, we must integrate them with other SEO tools, whether free or paid.

Ubersuggest

Ubersuggest is one of the greatest.

This is also a partially free tool that provides a wide range of SEO tips, and in my opinion, one of the best in terms of value for money (the free version already provides a lot of value, and the Premium options are definitely affordable - from 29 euros per month or 290 € in a single lifetime payment).

Also, it's one of the few free SEO analysis tools that not only supports keyword research but also basic on and off-site SEO analysis: simply log in with the site's Google account and you're done.

Moreover, among the free features is a hidden gem: the ability to download the Ubersuggest browser plugin, which makes standard Google searches interactive from an SEO standpoint. A really handy function that allows us to perform a brief Keyword analysis of what we are typing simply by typing in the search field.

In terms of keyword research, Ubersuggest provides more detailed information such as the number of people who really click on the SEO results, the age of the users, a wide range of keywords (related, suggested, queries, etc.), and, most importantly, a list of "content ideas." These are simply the first SERP results, displayed without the need for additional investigation, including information on projected visits, backlinks, and so on.

These features are typically only available in premium SEO Tools, thus it truly is a prized tool!

KWFinder

KWFinder is another intriguing tool for finding less common keywords with less competition.

It includes several truly unique and valuable features, such as the Link Profile Strength parameter (i.e. how many backlinks you would need for content with that keyword to make it to the front page).

This tool costs 29 euros each month.

How intelligent is Google?

As previously said, keyword research is only the first step in developing a good SEO plan.

Of course, choosing the appropriate keywords is essential if you want to rank high in Google SERPs, but you won't get very far if you don't include all of the other components of SEO. And there are a lot of them, as evidenced by the "Periodic Table of SEO Elements" below.

Google is becoming smarter, and it is relying less and less on SEO in the conventional sense to determine the quality of a piece of content and how much it deserves to be at the top of the SERP.

Using the appropriate keywords is vital, but it is not sufficient to ensure success. Google is now able to read more natural language and assess whether a piece of material genuinely answers a user's question or if it is full of keywords but has little value.

But how does it accomplish this? It employs an ever-expanding and more complex information system, which includes the elements listed in the periodic table.

It assesses not only text but also photos and other multimedia elements.

Sites that are speedy and load quickly should be rewarded.

To better comprehend the various components of the information, use code values such as schemas. Evaluate User Experience and Design

Assign a reputation value based on the age of the site, inbound links, and so on. And a variety of additional factors

It is obvious that handling SEO now increasingly entails having an integrated picture of the complete site in terms of what Google values.

However, the tools we've seen thus far are clearly insufficient to check all of these elements (links, structure, speed, mobile-friendliness, and so on): Heavy artillery, also known as Advanced SEO Tools, is required.

The whole suite of SEO tools for on-site and off-site SEO.

The tools for analyzing the Google website

Google, too, comes to our assistance with various free tools, specifically those used for website monitoring: Google Analytics and Google Search Console.

These two tools, especially when used together, allow you to thoroughly examine a site's performance in Google's eyes.

However, like with keyword research, the drawbacks of Google's SEO tools are twofold:

they are difficult to use at best

to collect complete data, numerous processes and several tools are required.

Google is working on it, and an upgrade called Search Console Insights will be available soon, providing an aggregate view of the data from the two sites.

For the time being, we may rely on complete SEO tools, which are programs that, in addition to allowing us to search for keywords, also assess our site and the numerous pages that comprise it to ensure that everything is in order. according to Google's specifications

These SEO Tools are nearly typically paid, although some of them offer a free version with limited functionality to sample or for people who only use these tools rarely.

Here are the most well-known.

Yoast is a WordPress SEO tester.

Yoast has become linked with SEO for good reason: their plugin is a must-have for anyone trying to handle on-page SEO on WordPress (the plugin is only available on this platform). Simply install it and, in its free version, it provides you with an overview of the SEO actions that need to be performed on a page in order to optimize it.

Its signature is the "traffic light": with this indicator, any content author can instantly determine whether his optimization is adequate, good, or exceptional.

In the Free version, YOAST allows you to enter a keyword per article and evaluate how many times it has been repeated, how many external and internal links there are, and so on, as well as easily and without accessing the code, modify parameters such as the META description, the SEO title, and so on.

The Premium edition (€ 89 per year) also allows you to optimize for numerous keywords (synonyms, related, etc.) and have access to sophisticated features such as automatic redirection of broken links (the dreaded "404 errors"), internal link suggestions, and much more.

SEMRush: The All-In-One Freemium SEO Tool

SEMRush is a top player in the SEO field: this tool allows you to analyze everything from SERP positions to inbound links, as well as site speed and broken links.

The system, which is already in its Free mode, assists you in creating a "project" and assesses your website in every way. Among the activities permitted by SEMRush are:

Domain analysis: traffic, backlinks, site authority, and so on.

Keyword analysis: all of the above-mentioned primary functions

Traffic analysis: audience, top pages, and so on.

Competitive analysis: which keywords are they positioned for, and so on

It is evident that it is much more than just an SEO tool; it is a really comprehensive website monitoring and analyzing environment.

A little difficult to use, but surely quite valuable, especially since the free edition of SEMRush allows you to access all of the site's functionalities for a restricted number of daily searches.

If you go over it, SEMRush has a number of premium subscriptions starting at € 99 per month.

Ahrefs is an SEO tool that focuses on backlinks.

Ahrefs is yet another comprehensive SEO analysis tool that offers much more than just aid with keyword research: its advanced monitoring system tracks not only your site to assure the best outcomes in terms of ranking, but also that of competitors.

In fact, it detects their backlinks and allows you to use them as a starting point for your SEO strategy, such as assisting you in understanding which material in your field obtains the most link.

Unfortunately, there is no free version in this situation, and the commercial plans are similar to those of SEMRush (the base plan costs € 99 per month).

On the other side, they provide a really important SEO tool for free, namely the Ahrefs Toolbar: comparable to the Ubersuggest extension, but with the extra benefit of data provided by a giant like Ahrefs!

Finally, how do you select the greatest SEO tool?

As you may have guessed, there is no such thing as a "best SEO Tool." You should try to figure out which one is best for you gradually.

If you are a content creator, you can settle for keyword research tools, possibly even free versions; however, if you have an online business or an eCommerce, you will almost certainly need to opt for a more comprehensive choice, which will help you not only choose the best keywords on which to position yourself, but also to keep the speed of the site under control, problems that may arise, competition, backlinks, and so on.

So I urge that you test them all (it's generally always easy to get a free one-week trial with all features unlocked) and see which one works best for you!

CHAPTER 2

SEM (SEARCH ENGINE MARKETING): A COMPLETE GUIDE TO SEARCH ENGINE MARKETING

The world of digital marketing is full of rules, methods, and, unfortunately, acronyms and acronyms to remember. SEM is one of these abbreviations. But what does that actually mean?

In English, Search Engine Marketing refers to all paid

digital marketing techniques aimed at increasing presence on search engines.

You are most likely already employing SEM methods without even recognizing it. Or perhaps you performed some web study to better comprehend us and ended up much more perplexed than before. In this chapter, I'll attempt to clear up any confusion.

So, let's take a look at what SEM is, how it may benefit your organization, and how to successfully execute a Search Engine Marketing strategy.

Definition of SEM

SEM is an abbreviation for Search Engine Marketing, which literally means "search engine marketing."

Brands use SEM to pay to have their advertising appear as search results on the SERP (the search results page).

You will select precise keywords, just as you would with SEO so that when a user searches for those phrases, they will see your brand ad right away.

Paid adverts can be found for practically any search query, usually at the top or bottom of the SERP. They are easily recognized from SEO-achieved positions since they carry the term "Ad" before the link.

In any case, in order to truly comprehend what SEM entails, it is vital to discuss its two key components, which are frequently muddled or misunderstood: SEO and SEA.

SEO + SEA = SEM

In reality, SEO and SEA methods are also classified as SEM. But what exactly are they?

SEO stands for search engine optimization (Search Engine Optimization), which is a method that tries to attain the highest possible positioning inside the SERP, or search engine results page, through the use of keywords. Research. SEO efforts take place both on-page and off-page (such as backlinks) and work together to get your site to the top of Google results.

SEA stands for Search Engine Advertising, and it is a type of digital marketing that focuses on promoting your business through tools like Google Ads.

As a result, we have stated that SEM is comprised of SEO and SEA. To beat Google's iconic first result, you'll need to work on both fronts, constantly optimizing your site and investing in sponsored techniques that will assist you in reaching your goal.

So, what is the distinction between SEO and SEM?

SEO encompasses all of the efforts required to improve your site so that it appears among the top results of search engines such as Google, whereas SEA is the process of directly promoting your (paid) site on search engines.

What exactly are SEM campaigns?

SEM efforts, which are related to your sponsored ad campaigns on search engines, are a terrific method to swiftly reach your potential clients.

SEM campaign ads show on Google and other search engines depending on the keywords you've chosen, and they reach the top of the results considerably faster than SEO campaigns.

But how exactly do SEM campaigns work?

Of course, you won't be the only one vying for first place, and Google will use criteria to choose which ads to display.

The three key factors that will influence your ranking are:

1. Keyword

2. Offering

3. The site's relevance

The easiest method to ensure the success of your SEM campaign is, to begin with, a clear aim in mind. What do you hope to accomplish? More visibility, traffic to your website, increased conversions, and increased sales? If your goal is clear, SEM can significantly boost your company's fortunes.

How much does Search Engine Marketing (SEM) cost?

When it comes to Search Engine Marketing and pricing, the important word is flexibility. It all relies on your budget and the goal you want to accomplish with your campaign.

The most critical consideration is your intended audience. What is the name of your buyer persona? Once you've identified your ideal customer, you can build customized marketing and campaigns to boost your chances of success.

It also evaluates alternative keywords and tactics to see what works best for your company. You may begin with a high-volume keyword only to discover that lower volume but greater conversion rate keywords are better for your business.

Certainly, you should be prepared to invest a little more money at the outset of your SEM adventure. In this manner, you can build a budget that is both reasonable and productive. Pulling on the pricing early on may result in a waste of time and money, and your efforts may still be unsuccessful.

Having said that, there are numerous tactics you may implement, such as paying only when a user clicks on your ad or based on the number of times your ad is viewed.

The benefits of SEM for your business

On our blog, we've already discussed how Google Ads can help your online store. Let's take a look at how SEM marketing can help your company expand faster.

SEM campaigns are an excellent approach to boosting your company's ROI; in fact, SEM accounts for the bulk of spending in online promotion activities.

SEM allows you to enhance your conversion rate by, for example, developing a landing page and promoting it using SEM. Your page will receive a lot of attention and will generate a lot of traffic and conversions.

Because of the ability to select a specific reference target, the leads generated by SEM campaigns are of high quality.

The results of SEM campaigns are quick and visible: you will never have to wait more than a day for your ad to be published.

If you want to advertise your business locally, SEM-sponsored ads might help you reach out to potential clients in your neighborhood.

SEM campaigns are relatively inexpensive, especially given that most advertisers believe that SEM returns much outweigh the costs.

SEM: Where does your ad show up?

Despite the fact that there are various alternatives to Google, the Big G remains a favorite among advertisers. So, let's take a look at the three main channels through which you might advertise your ad.

Search Network: When it comes to Search Engine Advertising, this is the most common network. It is primarily keyword-based and allows you to show your advertising when people are conducting research.

Display network: With this network, your adverts will appear in the form of text or banners on other websites that are part of the Google advertising circuit. The benefit of using this network is that you may target the users to whom you would show your adverts based on their interests or socio-demographic traits.

Video network: Similar to the display network, the video network allows you to communicate through video marketing on YouTube and other Google-affiliated video sites, while always focusing on your target demographic.

In addition, if you want to utilize SEM to sell your products, you can use the advertisements in the Google Shopping section. You can directly market the products you offer on this network, including the image, title, price, and store name.

Setting up a SEM strategy: What Tools Are Available?

You may feel like you're almost ready to launch your first SEM campaign at this point, but keep in mind that planning is crucial. And there are still some fundamentals you should understand before you begin promoting your business on search engines. Let's have a look at what they are.

Platforms for SEM

Search engines where you can market your adverts are referred to as "SEM platforms."

Google is unquestionably the most popular search engine, accounting for 92.4 percent of all browser searches.

You may still utilize other search engines, such as Bing, or go all-in on more specialized browsers, for example, if your target audience is located in a specific country.

Indeed, search engines primarily aimed at areas such as Russia or China have a far lesser number of competitors, and a lower number of competitors equates to a reduced cost for your SEM.

SEM Keyword Types

SEM keywords are the search terms that you will use in your SEM campaigns. These can be classified into four types:

Broad match keywords are those that seek variants on the search query. Similar sentences, multiple or singular versions, typing errors, or synonyms are examples.

For example, in addition to "virtual assistant," the SEM campaign can target "online assistants," "virtual teams," or "virtual assistants" for the "virtual assistant" search.

Phrase match: Targets the precise search phrase, plus any other phrases with words that before or follow the main keyword. For example, in addition to "virtual assistant," the SEM campaign can target "best virtual assistant," "online virtual assistant," or "hire a virtual assistant" for the "virtual assistant" search.

Identical match: Aims for a perfect match with the main term, allowing for minor variants such as typos, plural and singular forms, abbreviations, or paraphrases.

For example, in addition to "virtual assistants," the SEM campaign can target "virtual assistants," "virtual assistance," or "virtual assistants."

Reverse (negative) match: This sort of targeting excludes terms from your SEM campaign that you do not wish to include. As a result, it could be terms that are semantically comparable to your query but conceal a different search intent.

For example, the SEM campaign for "virtual assistants" may exclude "virtual assistant pay" or "virtual assistant training."

As you can see, the keywords you choose are heavily influenced by the goal of your SEM campaign.

SEM focusing

If keyword matching tells the search engine when to show your ads, targeting your SEM campaign allows you to select parameters that govern when, where, and to whom they are shown.

What are the parameters for ad targeting? Demographics: Information on the user's demographics. Affinity: Audiences that can be reached through search or display.

In-market: consumers looking for similar products and services to those advertised.

Intention: Tracks the user's search intent and assesses the possibility of them connecting with the ad.

Users with similar interests to those on your remarketing lists constitute a similar audience.

Users that have previously interacted with your adverts are referred to as remarketing. Computer, smartphone, tablet, or television screen

Your advertisement's copy

The majority of the elements of SEM ads correspond to the indexing of organic search results.

The following elements must be present in your ad:

Title

Display URL

Description

Site extensions

Your advertisement's auction

Setting up a SEM campaign does not guarantee that your advertisement will be seen by every user that searches for your keywords. SEM systems include algorithms that determine whether and when to show your ads, as well as how to make them compete with other advertising targeting the same keywords.

These algorithms function similarly to auctions and work as follows:

When a user searches, the platform system finds all advertising with matching keywords.

Ads that are ineligible (targeting another country or being rejected for various reasons) are ignored.

Only advertising with a relatively high ranking will be shown among the remaining ads.

Ranking is determined by a combination of the offer, quality, search intent, and the influence of extensions.

It is important to note that the person who makes the most offers does not always win. Even if one of your competitors buys higher than you, your ad will still rank higher due to the relevance and relevance of the keywords.

How to Improve SEM Outcomes

Because having a huge budget is not required to position your advertisements on the SERP, there are a number of things you can do to boost the outcomes of your SEM campaigns.

Look for the ideal keywords.

Using the correct keywords for your ads is critical to enhancing your ad rankings.

When looking for keywords, attempt to locate terms such as:

Keywords are used by your target audience: determine the most popular keywords, avoid overly formal language, and look for the most often used terms in your industry.

work at the bottom of your sales funnel - keywords searched by users at the bottom of your sales funnel are more likely to convert users.

are appropriate for your budget: if a keyword has a high search volume but is too expensive for your budget, look for more specialized phrases with a lower cost per click.

Make appealing advertisements.

Your SEM advertising, like organic search results, must not only exist on the SERP but also inspire consumers to interact with them.

That is why it is critical to focus on the content and organization of your advertisements.

Include the core keyword;

Communicate your message clearly and simply;

Write a description that matches the search purpose;

Include prices, discounts, or any specials (if relevant)

Include a clear call to action

Improve your current campaigns

Don't forget about your previous SEM initiatives! Even if your campaigns are already running, you should keep optimizing them.

You can perform a variety of things, such as add new relevant keywords, set negative keywords, or build alternative versions of your advertising for A / B tests and determine which works best for your audience.

SEM: the terms you absolutely must know the terms you must not overlook

There are some words that you will come across frequently during your SEM trip and that you must understand in order to manage your budget effectively.

PPC (Pay Per Click): PPC advertising is a sort of advertising in which you pay a fee every time your ad is clicked. When a user views your ad but does not click on it, an impression is still recorded.

CPA (Cost Per Acquisition): CPA is the cost of your PPC campaign divided by the number of conversions received. It will assist you in determining whether or not your campaign is providing a profitable ROI.

CPC (Cost Per Click): the price of each click in your SEM campaign. It is computed by dividing the ad ranks of your competitors by your Quality Score. It will assist you in determining how much to bid on an ad.

CPM (Cost per thousand impressions): This is the most frequent online advertising system, and it refers to the cost per thousand impressions of a banner ad on a web page.

You are now prepared to launch your first SEM campaign.

Search Engine Marketing is a highly successful method for increasing sales, promoting your company, and improving your internet visibility. The key advantage is that it allows you to show your adverts to highly interested customers at precisely the right time.

You now have all of the necessary credentials to launch your first SEM campaign and advertise your company to as many people as possible. Don't be discouraged if your initial attempts fail, and set a budget that corresponds to your capabilities.

You will see that results will appear, and your efforts will be rewarded - with interest!

CHAPTER 3

GOOGLE SERP: LEARN HOW TO APPEAR HIGHER ON GOOGLE

Search engine optimization (SEO) is essential for creating a traffic-generating ecommerce. Keeping up with all of the adjustments to search engine algorithms, on the other hand, is no easy task!

Especially since Google's algorithm changes on a daily basis.

Furthermore, Google's ten blue links no longer carry the traffic they once did.

Because? Because of the new SERP features.

These new SERP (search engine results page) elements have improved the user experience, but have made it much more difficult to rank on Google in the initial results.

And if you want to be at the top of the search results, you must completely comprehend the game's rules.

SERP: what it means

What do SERP and website indexing mean?

SERP is an abbreviation for search engine results page (s), which is derived from the English term "search engine results page (s)." As a result, it is nothing more than the engine's response in the search for a user.

Here's an example of a Google search engine result page:

SERP does not refer to a certain search engine.

SERPs are provided to users by Google, Bing, and Yahoo.

Today, no two SERPs are the same. Instead, each SERP is tailored to the individual user. This is why, when searching on different devices or from different places, you may see different search results.

What is the significance of the SERP?

Understanding what a SERP is is essential for learning how to rank high on Google. When it comes to SERPs, we place a high value on Google search engine optimization.

Because? Why Google is the undisputed king of search engines.

When was the last time you tried a different search engine? People no longer look for something "on the internet," but rather "on Google."

Take a look at these statistics as well.

In April 2019, Google accounted for 62.7 percent of all major searches in the United States, with Microsoft Sites accounting for 24.8 percent and Verizon Media (previously Oath and Yahoo) accounting for 11.6 percent.

And, once again, Google leads the US mobile search industry with a huge 93 percent market share.

But wait, there's more.

Google's domination is even more pronounced in many other large economies, such as the United Kingdom and Germany, where Google has a market share of 87-89 percent.

What function does the search engine result page (SERP) play in digital marketing?

SERP marketing is one of the marketing methods that focuses on promoting a firm within the search engine results. SERP marketing is classified into two types:

SEA SEO

To attain their business objectives, the most effective SERP marketing strategies combine SEO and SEA.

Let's have a look at these approaches:

What exactly is SEO?

SEO is an abbreviation for Search Engine Optimization, and it refers to the process of getting a high organic ranking in the SERP. Organic means you don't use any compensated approaches (like Google Ads).

There are numerous SEO methods and techniques available. Content marketing and backlink building are two of the most important strategies:

Material marketing is the creation of content with the goal of treating the primary issue of the major keyword in the most comprehensive way possible in order to be discovered by BigG.

Backlink profile: in a nutshell (although with a lot of effort), it implies becoming a point of reference important enough to receive external connections from other authoritative sites. This boosts domain authority and, as a result, search engine visibility.

The higher you rank in the SERP, the more clicks you'll receive.

SERP with graphics

The top five organic results on Google's first page account for more than 67 percent of first page clicks, whereas results 6 to 10 account for less than 4 percent.

Furthermore, top-tier organic content typically maintains its position in the SERPs for an extended period of time - without incurring the continuous expenditures associated with paid listings. In other words, it is a more long-term and sustainable marketing channel.

What exactly is the SEA?

SEA is an abbreviation for search engine advertising, and it refers to the practice of getting visitors from search engines via sponsored adverts and advertising. Google Ads is one of the most common SEA channels (formerly known as AdWords). These paid advertisements appear above and below organic search results, as well as in the sidebar, on Google. It is consequently critical to get to know them in order to understand how to boost a site's Google ranking.

Each paid ad is driven by specific keywords, and you typically pay for each click on each ad – hence the term pay-per-click, or PPC.

Google Ads are identified as paid advertisements by a small "Ads" badge, as shown in the example below:

While purchased results may not have the staying power of organic marketing, they may offer advantages.

For starters, you get a quicker return on investment (ROI).

With a well-targeted Google Ads campaign, you can quickly rise to the top of the SERPs and expose your company to new clients.

Furthermore, while paid results are unlikely to obtain the high clickthrough rate (CTR) that organic advertisements do, Google's PPC ads receive an average of 2% CTR and those who click on links frequently. They frequently become consumers.

But wait, there's more.

Paid results also include an analytics suite that shows you how to increase your CTRs and conversions. And this knowledge is priceless when it comes to optimizing SEO efforts.

As a result, the most effective SERP marketing incorporates both SEO and SEA.

What exactly are SERP features?

A SERP feature is any type of search engine page result that is not a regular organic result. These improvements are intended to improve the user experience by tailoring each SERP to provide more relevant and informative information.

Here's what Google's organic search results looked like a decade ago to help you grasp the power of SERP functions:

Obviously, a lot has changed.

Google's SERPs are now far more informative, relevant, and accurate. Google is attempting to lower the amount of time and effort required for users to locate what they are looking for, and every business must keep up.

In 2022, the Google SERP feature will be available.

Google is continually updating and adding new elements to the SERP. This means that there are various approaches to get your company to the top of the search engine results pages

(SERPs) today.

Here's a quick rundown of Google's SERP features in 2020: Rich Response

Rich Answers are sometimes referred to as answer boxes, rapid answers, and direct answers. These are frequently displayed in SERPs for simple queries such as "what time is it in the UK?" and "what is a steam engine?"

Google does not attribute Rich Answer sources because the information is in the public domain, according to Google.

Exceptional Outcome

A Rich Result (formerly known as a Rich Snippet) is comparable to a standard Google SERP result, except it provides more information than the title, meta description, and URL. Customer reviews, pricing, or links are frequently used as additional information.

Website owners can optimize their content for Google Rich Results by including structured data.

Card of Wealth (mobile)

Rich Cards are the smartphone version of Rich Results. Because the majority of Google searches are conducted on mobile devices, it is critical to developing a strategy that is tailored to these devices and the individuals that use them.

Mobile Knowledge Cards SERP

Knowledge Cards function similarly to Rich Cards, with

the exception that they are based on specific data. For example, if you search for "Italy population," you will see the following Knowledge Graph:

Graph of Knowledge

Because these are dependent on specific data, it is very challenging to fill these positions in the SERP.

Graph of Knowledge

Knowledge Graphs appear above organic results or in the right sidebar. They frequently feature photos, data, maps, and research ideas. This SERP function is frequently displayed for questions regarding specific topics, places, or persons.

Google takes information from its data from services such as Google Maps as well as external sources such as Wikipedia to generate Knowledge Graphs.

Panel of Experts

Knowledge Panels are nearly identical to Knowledge Graphs, with the exception that Google only gets data from Google Maps or Google My Business. As a result, Knowledge Panels appear for questions concerning brands, companies, or organizations.

Images, statistics, social media links, and related studies are frequently included in Knowledge Panels.

3-Pack Local

A Local 3-Pack is a SERP feature that includes a map as

well as a list of three local businesses, such as Rich Results. Local 3-packs are typically displayed when inquiries concerning local businesses or organizations are asked. Users looking for local businesses frequently have a high level of commercial intent. As a result, being in a Local 3-pack can do wonders for attracting new clients.

Map of SERPs

Please keep in mind that this SERP feature is only available for businesses having physical locations.

Panel of buyers

When looking for things to buy, Google Shopping appears on the SERP in the form of a dedicated panel. A carousel of photographs of the searched object appears, along with some facts such as the dealer site, the price, and a brief description.

Google Shopping Panel SERP functionality

This SERP feature appears for any search that has images or could benefit from visual results. Images appear in about 23% of Google's SERPs, and this figure is growing.

Unfortunately for businesses, when a user clicks on an image, they are directed to Google Images rather than the website from whence the image originated.

Video

Google will also display a series of three YouTube videos on occasion. A search for "how to change a tire" yields three thumbnail videos, which visitors may browse through to see other similar videos.

A website link

This SERP tool displays a collection of links from a specified domain. When a user searches for a specific organization or website, webpage links are typically displayed. Google's goal is to guide users to the web page they are looking for.

People have also inquired

The "People also asked" area contains similar questions to help users delve further into a topic. These options are quite prevalent and are frequently displayed for general research or direct inquiry.

SERP-related queries

There are tools available to help you identify the various queries offered in this area for a certain term. Also Ask is the easiest to use (and it's free).

Twitter This SERP feature is a collection of three of a Twitter account's most recent tweets. Tweets that are displayed may contain photos and links. Users can also access more tweets from the account by swiping right.

Main news This SERP feature displays the most recent news or trending stories connected to a search. Google offers three primary stories, each with a title, image, link, and the date the piece was published.

Featured snippet

Google's Featured Snippets are commonly referred to as 'position 0' because they are the best approach for businesses to acquire organic visibility in the SERPs.

What exactly is a snippet?

When it comes to Google SERPs, one word that always emerges is a snippet. But what exactly does snippet mean? The literal meaning is "fragment," hence when this term is used in programming, it refers to a code fragment. However, when it comes to Google positioning and SERPs, the phrase snippet has a distinct connotation.

The Google snippet is a preview of the web page content, and ideally, a well-optimized snippet provides the reader with enough information to be happy with the response while also leaving an atmosphere of interest that pushes the user to click on it. Click on that link to learn more. Here is the SERP's amazing potential.

According to Ahrefs, 99.58 percent of featured snippets are pulled from pages that are already in the top ten of the search engine results pages. As a result, in order to have a chance at ranking zero, businesses must already be at a prominent position in the SERPs.

Paragraphs

Google pulls text and sometimes an image from a page to build paragraphs in an attempt to answer the user's question directly within the SERPs.

This is the most common sort of featured snippet, and these paragraphs are frequently displayed for questions that begin with "how to do it," "what is it," or "why."

According to recent news, Google has begun a series of trials that include adding external links within the snippet. In practice, choose sources relating to our topic and place backlinks within the snippet's chosen paragraph.

In addition, a feedback request has been added. In essence, the user is asked to assess the usefulness of the text in the zero position. This emphasizes the importance of optimizing blog content from a snippet standpoint.

Lists with numbers

This SERP function usually ranks items numerically or lists directions on how to perform something.

Lists with bullets

This search function is nearly identical to the numbered list, with the exception that it is merely bulleted. These snippets are frequently displayed for unranked lists, and the content displayed is frequently pulled from articles.

Tables This SERP function displays photos on a table that also contains data like statistics and rankings.

The size and structure of these tables frequently change depending on the search request. Google can also take data from other sources to generate its own table.

YouTube

This SERP feature is derived from YouTube and

frequently displays a specific video clip. YouTube snippets are frequently used to answer "how-to" questions or any other questions that are best addressed in video form.

Carousel Google's carousel function suggests keywords that are related to the one we looked for.

scholarly papers

Scientific or academic articles may also appear in the Google SERPs in a dedicated section. When you Google "startups and psychology," you'll find the following results:

Academic publications from SERP

Articles from scientific journals and other publications will be published here.

Scroll down to the bottom of the SERP to discover related search recommendations. These are Google's suggestions based on the user's own research. If Google can't locate anything by the conclusion of the page, it takes a different strategy.

Google-related searches Tip: Use this function while deciding on keywords and content strategy.

Review

We also have a review of the SERP features. There are two kinds of it:

Evaluation of a business: this usually appears if your company is listed on Google My Business.

Evaluation of a product or service: There are several review sites, such as MyMovies, that use stars in SERPs to express their opinion about a film. The same is true in the publishing industry, for example.

Google SERP paid feature in 2022

Now that we've covered all of the major organic SERP features, let's take a look at the two types of paid features for Google's SERP in 2020.

Google Ads (formerly AdWords)

These ads are created with Google Ads, and businesses can use them to target specific keywords. They look almost identical to regular ads but include a small "Ad" badge before the URL.

The four most coveted advertising positions are above organic results at the top of the SERPs.

However, Google also displays paid listings under the organic results at the bottom of the page. Understandably, these get fewer clicks and, as a result, are less expensive to buy.

Google Shopping

The second partially paid feature of the SERP is Google Shopping. This is returned for searches that are highly related to the products, and these users typically have high commercial intent.

Why in part? Because since April 2020, Google has opened Organic Shopping (here to learn more) (here to learn more).

Paid shopping results consist of product listings. Each listing usually contains the product title, image, seller's name, and customer ratings.

They often appear at the top of the SERPs, above the organic results:

Organic and paid Google shopping

How to appear high on the Google SERP

So what are the tools to appear high on the SERP?

1. Organic Search Engine Optimization (SEO) (SEO)

2. Paid Search Engine Marketing (SEA) (SEA)

What are the features of the Google SERP in 2022?

Rich Answer

Rich Result

Rich Card

Knowledge Cards

Knowledge Graph

Knowledge Panel

Local 3-Pack

Shopping Panel

Image Pack

Link to the site

People have also asked

Twitter

Main news

Featuredsnippet

Academic articles

Related searches

Review

By now you should have understood by now what SERP, SEO, and SEA are, and what are the various Google SERP features available.

The best SERP marketing strategies use the two together to maximize traffic.

CHAPTER 4

OPTIMIZATION FOR SEARCH ENGINES

SEO optimization for freelancers with their own blog and website SEO is an abbreviation for Search Engine Optimization.

If you have updated the layout and graphics of your website, you will absolutely improve the entire experience that the user will have while landing on your web pages, and you will undoubtedly offer a very good impression of yourself and your organization.

However, web design alone will not help you rank on Google and allow your consumers to find you. We mostly talk about Google because it is the most popular search engine.

So, what does it mean to optimize your website? What exactly are SEO for a website and a blog?

The subject is vast, and there are numerous variables that can help with SEO optimization.

Because the web is now so rich in material, optimizing your site from an SEO standpoint is not an easy or quick process, and it is never conclusive!

People are at the heart of everything.

In practice, SEO optimization entails ensuring that your website offers the best response to the queries and problems that users in your industry are searching for online.

If you work in the kitchen industry, for example, a user could search Google for "vegetarian recipes" and find a post on your site in the SERP, or search results, because you discussed numerous vegetarian menus on your blog. You are providing relevant and high-quality content on this topic, which is most likely already being accessed by others.

First and first, you must concentrate on people and what they are looking for.

Responding to their needs must be your focus and objective since it is also Google's goal. And it will continue to be so, regardless of changes and improvements to Google's algorithms (which, believe me, are often!).

As a result, you must consider them before Google when dealing with SEO optimization.

Are keywords the answer?

You've most likely heard of it. When we think about SEO, we automatically think of the well-known keywords, as if they were the panacea for all placement issues.

In actuality, they are one of several factors to consider, and while important, they do not always guarantee you the desired position.

The reason is simple: the competition is so fierce right now that it will be impossible, especially if your site is new, to get by simply by studying and employing keywords well.

Keywords are also used in search engine optimization, which are the terms that users search for online when they want to find an answer or a solution to their questions.

Keywords with a long tail

If you've never done this before, it may appear to be a straightforward process, but it's not. First and foremost, you must remove your job clothing and put yourself in the shoes of your clients, using the same terms they would use if they were seeking a similar issue to yours.

Some of my clients frequently provide me with a single keyword or, in any event, a group of very broad keywords for their websites. In reality, that is the simplest thought that comes to mind; unfortunately, it is not the correct one.

Using a hypothetical cooking blog as an example, it will be extremely tough to position oneself well for the dry keyword "kitchen" because online competition is already intense and there are far more authority sites in the industry that utilize it.

Instead, research so-called long-tail keywords, which are significantly more specialized and are based on a sentence rather than a single word.

For example, if we're talking about a culinary blog, you might consider utilizing the long tail keyword "recipe for a vegetarian Christmas meal" or "how to prepare a vegetarian first dish for Christmas" for your content.

How can I locate keywords?

There are various internet resources that can assist you.

One of them is Ubersuggest, which is free and allows you to search for comparable terms while automatically adjusting to your language.

However, be cautious: being clever with Google is never a good idea! So avoid keyword stuffing, or stuffing your web page with terms. Not only would it degrade your users' reading experience, but the search engine will respond by perceiving the unjustifiable and forced profusion of keywords as spam.

How can you tell if you typed your term naturally?

Continue reading!

A plugin for SEO

If you use WordPress, there are various plugins that can assist you with SEO.

The finest two are Yoast SEO and All in One SEO Pack, both of which are available in a freemium, or partially free, edition.

I've tested both of them and prefer Yoast. Yoast's free version already includes a number of useful features for improving your SEO optimization.

Don't expect a plugin to perform everything on its own while you sip your tea and do something else once you've installed and activated it. Yoast, for example, works great provided you use it appropriately, which means entering the starting keyword, a meta description, the alt tag of the photos, and a featured image, among other things...

It also reports the keyword density (which we discussed briefly before), whether it is sufficient in percentage or if it should also be included in the headings.

So considering using a plugin is a good idea, as long as you implement it and work on it on a regular basis.

The rate of loading

However, SEO optimization is more than just a matter of keywords.

In truth, several factors influence SEO, such as your site's loading speed.

If your website is slow, users are more inclined to abandon it.

If you consider that the majority of browsing is now done on mobile devices, you realize that waiting times are critical since your consumers do not want to wait and spend time to acquire the information they require.

They simply leave your site and go to your competitor's, increasing the bounce rate.

The bounce rate informs Google that your web page has been abandoned by your users, which could lead the search engine to consider it dull and of low quality.

You can use Google's Page Performance to assess the speed of your web pages, which also provides ideas and tactics for perhaps improving the speed of a page on your site.

Using excessively large photos also slows down the display.

Make sure that the visual content accompanying your articles and pages has good compression and is thus easily accessible while being pleasant and relevant to the topic.

Another crucial issue that might affect the speed of your site is the type of hosting you have acquired for it.

Image optimization

It is critical to select and integrate images to accompany your information. Images not only aid in the reading of pages and articles by compelling the reader to linger on your material, but they can also help you rank higher on Google if you optimize them for SEO.

In principle, using original photographs, perhaps captured expressly for your online project or graphics, would be the ideal option. In theory, I say, because in practice, it is not always possible, let alone simple (not for everyone, at least).

First and foremost, give the photographs you are about to post to your site a clever name, ensuring that the search key of the referring content is included. As a result, avoid names like image123.jpg or something similar.

Also see: WordPress Featured Image Insertion

If your article's keyword is "free beaches in Sardinia," and you talk about the greatest beaches to go to the water in Sardinia without paying a ticket, your image will be labeled, for example, beaches-free-in-Sardinia-August-2018.png.

At the same time, remember to always include the alt tag when embedding it in your text.

The alt tag or alt text, which you can simply complete if you use WordPress, must be descriptive text for the image that includes the reference keyword.

You can also include an image description if it makes sense in that context, i.e. if the goal is to improve the browsing experience and boost the value of the content.

If the image is only the cover of an article or page, you may wish to skip the caption. You might want to include it if it's practical, such as displaying something unique and taking up some space on the page.

SEO optimization (on-page and off-page)

To summarize, working on your website's SEO is crucial since it provides free visibility and advertising (depending on how you do it, of course), but the effects of your efforts do not appear fast. They are a matter of time and also rely on consistent and continual work.

You did an excellent job on your most recent piece, seeking evidence to back up your claims and providing entertaining images and videos to your readers. You've also invested effort in determining your target's keywords. Unfortunately, this work is insufficient.

CHAPTER 5

META DESCRIPTION: HOW TO WRITE THEM AND WHY THEY MATTER

If you own an ecommerce business, you must do everything necessary to promote your online store. You've probably heard of SEO optimization and words like meta title, meta description, and so on. These tactics can be used to drive organic traffic to your online store.

You may have already begun optimizing other areas of your business, like product text and images, but you may be struggling to optimize your meta descriptions.

What exactly is a meta description?

A meta description is a text snippet that summarizes a page's content.

It's a "meta tag," which is an HTML element utilized by both users and search engines to determine what they'll find when they click on the link. It is also referred to as the page's "snippet."

The description meta tag, along with the meta title and other "meta" components, is one of the features to improve while doing SEO by entering the main keyword.

How many characters should a meta description have?

The meta description can be up to 160 characters long.

In actuality, because the number of visible characters is not fixed but is determined by the size of the individual letters (an "m" takes up more space, or pixels, than an I it is best to position between 150 and 160 characters to avoid truncations.

How does the meta description appear in HTML code and on the page?

The meta description is a line of code that looks something like this:

code for meta description example

Do you think it's Arabic? It is, in fact, another language, a computer language. But don't worry, all you have to do is write in your language in the area devoted to your management system's Meta Description.

You've most likely seen some meta descriptions on the Google search results page.

When you type a search term into Google, you will be greeted with a SERP (search results page). On this SERP, you will see a variety of results linked to your search.

There are two key features that you will notice. The first element is the blue text known as the 'Title Tag.' The Title Tag's role is to display the page's title.

The meta description is located below and serves a straightforward purpose: it informs visitors and encourages them to click on your link.

Why are meta descriptions important?

As a business owner, you will want to do everything possible to get your items in front of potential clients. Meta descriptions aid in increasing click-through rates from three major sources: search engine results, social media sharing, and social bookmarks.

A meta description can provide more information about the page and assist attract the reader's attention to all three of these sources.

Although search engines have stated that meta descriptions are not directly used in the ranking algorithm, Google analyzes a website's CTR (Click Through Rate) to determine how well your web page matches the search query. Because meta

63

descriptions can enhance your page's CTR, they are an excellent approach to improving your Google rating.

More visitors will come to your website if you rank higher on Google. More people visiting your store equals more prospective consumers, which means you'll have a better chance of making sales. After all, Google has an estimated 1.6 billion active users, so the potential is enormous!

What is a meta description?

Now that we've defined a snippet, let's look at how to create a meta description that will generate more visitors to your online business. It is vital to note that the meta descriptions for a home page and product pages differ slightly. We've produced a basic method for producing meta descriptions for both home pages and product pages, which you can find below:

Make a home page SEO meta description.

When crafting a meta description for your homepage, you must convey your company's main message in no more than 160 characters. Even if you are an experienced copywriter, this is a difficult task.

As a general rule, keep the meta description as basic as feasible while yet offering a compelling incentive to click on the page.

When your prospects utilize Google, they won't even comprehend why they choose you; they'll simply see a captivating snippet and click on the link.

Here's a wonderful example of a meta description for a home page:

Adidas surely does not require an introduction, and they have produced a meta description that entices consumers shopping for sportswear to click on their link. It targets its audience directly, saying "Find Adidas shoes and clothing," and encourages the user to buy by offering free returns for 100 days.

Make a product page's SEO meta description.

Writing a meta description for a product page differs slightly from writing a meta description for a home page. Instead of communicating your brand's vision in only 160 characters, you must persuade potential buyers of the benefits they will receive if they click on your product page.

It's a good idea to add your product's strengths in the meta description because this will attract more potential buyers.

Here's a wonderful example of a product page meta description:

Example of a meta description for an SEO product

The meta description for Isaac's Baladin beer is shown in this sample. The product and keyword are both listed in the meta description, which is excellent for SEO optimization.

Following that, the following information is provided to help frame the product: Color, flavor, and spiciness... In a nutshell, anything that would be of interest to a person looking for a beer.

You can use these samples as inspiration when writing a meta description for your shop's home page or a best-selling product page.

You can alter the meta descriptions in Shopify's settings if you run your store with Oberlo.

You may get to it from your Sales Channel by clicking on Pages and then 'Edit Website SEO.'

Don't worry if you haven't yet created meta descriptions for your web pages; Google will build one for you.

The Google algorithm will simply take the text that is already on your website to generate meta descriptions.

While employing these auto-generated meta descriptions may suffice, it is your responsibility as an ecommerce entrepreneur to ensure that your store stands out from the throng.

Create accurate meta descriptions and you will be able to enhance your CTR and further optimize the page for a specific keyword.

Tools for previewing meta descriptions

Before publishing the page, use a meta description preview tool to see how your snippet would appear on a SERP. These tools are crucial if you want to improve the SEO of your website.

Here are a few free meta description preview tools to help you fine-tune your snippets.

Portent has designed a simple meta description preview tool that you can use to inspect and improve the meta descriptions of your pages. When using this tool, enter the title tag, meta description, URL, and any keywords you want to optimize. After you enter this information, you will be shown how the page would appear on a SERP.

To The Web To TheWeb offers two aspects that are both beneficial to an ecommerce business. The first function allows you to enter the page's URL to see how it would appear on a SERP. The tool's second feature is a meta description editor, which you can use to alter and optimize your page's meta description. Once you've created an ideal meta description, you can reload your website and begin enjoying the benefits of your efforts.

Create meta descriptions that are mobile-friendly.

When it comes to optimizing a website for search engines, it is critical to consider the mobile audience. It is believed that mobile devices account for over 60% of all Google search inquiries and that this proportion will only rise.

It's a good idea to keep this in mind while you write meta descriptions for your pages. We recommend creating your WordPress meta descriptions with Yoast, which allows you to see your desktop and mobile snippets.

6 hints for improving your snippets

Congratulations, you are now ready to begin developing your meta descriptions!

Whether you're an experienced SEO writer or this is your

first time optimizing a website, you'll discover the finest writing strategies as you build your snippets.

Before you begin producing meta descriptions, consider the following six recommendations to help you improve your meta descriptions and increase your store's CTR:

Answer the following user question: To get answers to their questions, people use search engines such as Google. It doesn't matter if the user's question is "Is it hot in Berlin in the summer?" or "How to Get Rich With Dropshipping?" If you can answer the user's question in your meta descriptions, you can persuade curious readers to click on your material.

Make certain that your meta descriptions are relevant: When crafting a meta description, make sure the material is relevant not only to the Title Tag but also to the search phrase the user is looking for. If you sell sunglasses and your meta description includes information about bags, your viewers will be perplexed and reluctant to click on your website.

Get your point across: When it comes to meta descriptions, 160 characters isn't much to work with. Once you've settled on the message you want to express, try to fit as much of it as you can inside the character restriction. Every word should have a purpose, and that purpose should be to increase your CTR.

Make a Captivating Title Tag: Several studies demonstrate that if you have intriguing text, 8 out of 10 viewers will click on your page. Use this information to generate eye-catching headlines for your websites. They will significantly assist your store in generating and securing traffic.

Use CTAs to your advantage: It's a good idea to include a CTA (Call To Action) in your meta description. A CTA such as 'Buy Now' is a straightforward instruction that can compel your users to act and buy a product from your store.

Utilize active verbal forms: When creating meta descriptions, it is always ideal to use the active voice. Instead of saying "Find all the best styles here," say "Find all the best styles here." In this manner, you will convey a demand to potential clients rather than a suggestion.

You are now prepared to develop flawless meta descriptions for your online store! Use the strategies and tricks in this chapter to start producing more organic traffic for your ecommerce site right away.

CHAPTER 6

WHAT ARE GOOGLE ADS AND HOW CAN THEY ASSIST YOUR ONLINE STORE?

If you run an ecommerce shop and aren't already using Google Ads, which helps you to develop your brand and attract new consumers by advertising on websites and search engines, you're missing out on something incredible.

Don't put it off any longer; after reading this chapter, you will undoubtedly be able to put it to good use!

But what exactly is Google Ads, and how does it work?

What exactly are Google Ads?

Google Ads was introduced shortly after Google.com become the world's most popular website. In fact, the American behemoth launched its paid advertising business Google Adwords in 2000, which was rebranded as Google Ads in 2018.

Google Ads and Google Adwords are thus the same things, or rather the first is a new brand that contains everything that was previously available.

But what exactly are Google Ads?

It is basically a network of paid adverts displayed on Google channels, ranging from the search results page (SERP) to websites that have agreed to display the platform's ads, from YouTube to Gmail, and so on.

With Google being the behemoth that it is, it is a multidimensional advertising system that is complete, dependable, and relatively easy to utilize.

Google Ads is a paid platform that falls within the marketing category of "pay-per-click," literally translated into "pay-per-click" in English.

It boils down to this: the advertiser, or whoever publishes the ad (in fact, the ad), pays for each click or impression acquired by the ad.

But how does it work in practice?

How Does Google Ads Work?

To understand this service, simply stating that it is a PPC (pay-per-click) platform is insufficient.

To begin understanding how Google Ads works, you must first determine what Google Ads is for.

Google Ads is a highly successful approach to drive high-quality, interested traffic to your website. The traffic that comes to your website as a result of this platform will be made up of potential clients who are already looking for items and services comparable to those supplied by your business.

As a result of Google Ads, you can improve traffic to your website, attract more potential consumers, and increase visits to your physical store, if you have one.

But, in order to fully comprehend what Google Ads can achieve for your company, we must first examine the platform's technical components as well as the various alternatives offered to marketers.

Where can I find Google Ads?

When you think of Google, you probably think of the well-known search engine, right? And, in reality, one of the available Google Ads placements is precisely among the well-known results.

However, it is not the only option; quite the opposite. Google Ads can be found on:

Search Network: presented at the top or bottom of the SERP, preceded by the Ad disclaimer, they appear in all respects as organic search results, with the exception of a few additional features that we shall see shortly.

Shopping Ads are a subset of Google Ads for the Search network that appear in both a dedicated "Google Shopping" tab in the search engine and a prominent strip at the top before the organic results.

Display Network: These adverts, which take the shape of graphic and/or textual banners, can be found on the millions and millions of websites that are part of the partner network and have agreed to exhibit Google Ads advertisements.

Gmail advertisements, which are expandable and interactive adverts that display as emails in Gmail, are found in the Promotions and Social folder.

Shopping ads on Google ads

Finally, video ads are available for YouTube, smart TV, and other video formats.

You may also use Smart Campaigns or Discovery to combine several formats.

Google Ads campaigns are classified into several types.

The numerous sorts of Google Ads campaigns available to you are determined by the goals you wish to achieve:

Brand awareness and notoriety: making the company known to as many potential customers as possible.

Brand Consideration: When analyzing a purchase, recall the brand's memory.

Traffic: the purpose is to direct users to the landing page.

Lead generation: you only pay when the goal of acquiring contacts is met.

Conversion: The purchase of a product is referred to as a conversion.

App promotion: promoting the download of an app.

Local shop visits: for Google My Business local pages.

The cost of Google Ads, the metrics to consider when evaluating success, and many other things that we will examine together will all be affected by all of the choices.

The Advantages of Using Google Ads

The biggest advantage of using Google Ads for your ecommerce is that when people search for something on Google, they are looking for something particular.

In the context of ecommerce, it indicates they have already decided to buy and have thus entered the sales funnel. They are actively seeking to purchase a product or service.

And they're essentially telling Google what kind of product or service they're looking for by typing relevant terms into the search field.

That is why Google Ads is such a great ecommerce tool. Even if your ecommerce does not rank among the top Google results organically, thanks to your SEO efforts and Google Ads, all Google users who are looking for a product or service that is similar to your ecommerce will see your site in their SERP.

However, the advantages of Google advertising do not stop there:

Budget control: With Google Ads, you can always decide on the daily or total budget to commit to a campaign based on your KPIs and, most importantly, the goals you want to achieve.

Speed of results: It is very simple to test and deploy campaigns on Google Ads because the results are visible in real-time or practically real-time, and you can easily alter your tactics.

Relevance of the target: Whether you choose the Search network or the Display network, the individuals who view your advertising will be completely relevant: they are users who have typed in keywords related to your product or service or have demonstrated an active interest in something comparable.

Which Is Better for Your Business: Google Ads or Facebook Ads? The primary distinction between Google Ads and Facebook Ads or

Instagram advertising differs from Google Ads in that it shows your ad to people who are already interested in the products or services you sell on your website.

In contrast, with a Facebook ad, your ad will appear in the feed of a specific set of individuals who may be potential buyers for your ecommerce but aren't actively looking to buy your product or service.

To attract visitors who view your ad within your sales funnel and, as a result, your website, you will need to apply several marketing methods on Facebook.

What is the cost of Google Ads?

The good news is that the cost of Google ads is totally determined by your budget, how much you want or can invest, and the objectives you've set.

Because this is a PPC platform, the cost of each ad is connected to the number of clicks or whatever action or objective you have selected.

Google Advertising provides many bidding choices for your ads based on your ecommerce goals.

For example, if you sell a cycling accessory on your ecommerce site, your primary goal will most likely be to attract as many customers as possible. Instead, if you manage a bicycle club, you may want to expand the number of people on your email list.

So, here are the offers that you may use to establish a **Google Ads campaign.**

The cost per click (CPC)

If you select to pay per click, you will only be charged for the clicks on your adverts.

You'll need to set a maximum CPC, which is the maximum cost you'll be paid for a click, and every time someone clicks on your ad, you'll know that the click will never cost you more than the maximum CPC you've set.

You can also select between manual and automatic bidding. Manual bidding allows you to select the bidding amounts, whereas automatic bidding allows Google to set the bids to get you the most clicks while staying within your budget.

By dividing the entire cost of clicks by the total number of clicks, you can figure the average amount you will have to spend for a click on your ad.

For example, if your ad receives two clicks, one at € 0.20 and one at € 0.40, your average CPC will be € 0.30, which is calculated by dividing € 0.60 (the total cost of clicks) by two (the total number of clicks).

You may calculate the average amount you might be charged for each click using Google's Keyword Planner.

Price per impression

If you want to boost the visibility of your ecommerce through Google Ads, you can prioritize impressions (the total number of views) over clicks.

Google will adjust your bids to reach your impression target in this manner.

For example, if you select a top-of-page impression share of 65 percent, Google will ensure that your advertisements display at the top of the SERP in 65 percent of cases.

As a result, you will be charged based on the number of times your ad displays prominently, and you will be charged per 1000 times your ad appears as visible by Google users.

The cost of each action (CPA)

If increasing your ecommerce conversion rate is your primary goal, you can prioritize conversions.

Conversion in Google Ads is any action you want people to do on your website. It could be a purchase, but it could also be a newsletter subscription or something else.

You will continue to pay per click, but by prioritizing conversions, Google will adjust your bids to make as many acquisitions as feasible, always based on the cost per action required by your budget.

This type of offer is slightly more advanced, and in order

to track the correct progress of this Google Ads campaign, you must also use Conversion Tracking, a free tool that helps you understand which ads are most effective for your ecommerce and in which measuring your ad clicks are driving the actions that matter to you.

The cost per view

The latter type of offer is exclusively available for video commercials.

You can prioritize views if your main purpose is to track the level of interaction with your material.

With this package, you will only be charged for video views and activities performed by people on your video, such as clicks on tabs or banners.

How much does Google advertising cost? It is determined by the auction mechanism.

The preceding will establish your bidding strategy, i.e. your campaign bidding strategy.

But, more specifically, given that you are unlikely to be the only person interested in ranking for a specific phrase and that there are only a few paid positions (typically 2-4), how does Google pick who to rank in response to a given search / in a specific position?

Simple: through the auction system, which the algorithm executes in a few thousandths of a second depending on the predetermined ad rating.

As with any auction, the highest bidder wins, therefore setting a reasonable maximum CPA (cost per action) is critical.

But that's not all; there are other factors that influence the auction outcome. The position you will receive and the amount you will pay is determined by the Ad Rank, which is governed by six factors:

Your bid: The most you're willing to spend for a click on your ad.

The relevance and usefulness of your ad and the website to which it directs the person who will view the ad: Google Ads considers the relevance and usefulness of your ad and the website to which it links the person who will see the ad (evaluation enclosed in the elusive quality score, a number you can track and try to improve in your Google Ads account).

Thresholds for Ad Rank: There are minimum quality thresholds that an ad must meet in order to be shown.

The level of competition in an auction: highly competitive keywords typically have a higher minimum CPA.

The user's search context is examined, which includes the search terms entered by the user, the user's geographical location at the time of the search, the type of device used (for example, mobile or desktop), the search time, the nature of the search terms, other ads and search results displayed on the page, and additional user attributes and indicators.

Ad extensions and alternative ad formats are projected to have the following impact: When you build your ad, you may add more information to it, such as your phone number or other connections to specific pages on your site (extensions), which affect the user experience that your ad provides and thus the final rating.

How to Make Use of Google Ads

As you may be aware, Google Ads allows you to create and share adverts, both on desktop and mobile, that will be seen by your target market across many channels.

These are exceptional opportunities to be discovered by the proper audience and convert the conversion you have set as your objective.

But how does it work? What am I able to accomplish with Google Ads? How can I make effective advertisements?

We'll go through how to join up for Google Ads and establish a campaign on this platform in detail below.

How can I register for Google Ads?

Signing up for and using Google Ads is a breeze.

The only prerequisite is that you have a Gmail email account. Simply click on the following link to create a profile on the Google Ads platform: https://ads.google.com/intl/it it/home/

Simply pick the nation, time zone, and currency, then enter our personal information, agree to the terms and conditions, and finally check the email address.

When your Google Ads account is activated, you will be able to enter your billing information in the gear icon menu.

So, we're all set to launch our first Google Ads campaign!

Step-by-step instructions for creating a Google Ads campaign

Based on what we've seen so far, the first step is to establish what the primary target of your Google Advertising ads will be.

The second step will be to specify where you want your advertising to appear:

The guided choice alternatives will vary depending on the selected settings, but in general, all of the parameters displayed above can be adjusted in the following screen:

Locality;

Languages;

Audience segments;

Budget;

Bidding strategy;

Ad extensions.

Create google ads campaign

The next steps will be to create ad groups, creatives (texts and/or graphics depending on the type of positioning chosen), and ultimately to analyze the results.

Your ad (or ads, if you've chosen to create more than one) will be displayed to Google users who search for services or goods comparable to those specified in your campaign and on your website.

Is the Google Ads campaign failing? Here's what you should do. There are a number of reasons why your Google Ads campaign may fail.

The following are some of the more common causes:

Keywords that are too broad

The keywords for which you optimize your campaign must be as specific as possible, otherwise, you risk Google exposing your ad to the wrong target, resulting in fewer clicks and a greater cost. Worse, you could be penalized at the all-important Quality Score level!

Never stop tracking the progress of your campaigns and experimenting with new keywords until you find the ones that work best for your brand.

Advertisements that are irrelevant

If your ad does not match people's searches, you will not receive enough clicks to cover the cost of the ad. Your ad's headline and description should match the keywords you're employing, and it should also be evident to the user that clicking on your ad will lead them to a solution to their problem or an answer to their inquiry.

The landing page is not optimized.

It is not only the advertisements that must be effective. What do potential buyers view after clicking on your link? If your landing page is not optimized, i.e. it does not employ the same keywords as the ad, or your link goes to something completely different than the ad, the user will feel befuddled (or worse, mocked) and will exit your website without taking any action. Google will use this information to adversely appraise your ad and hinder its performance.

A low-quality rating

A quality Score is an estimate of the quality of your site, advertisements, and keywords. The higher the quality, the lower the cost, and the higher the visibility of your Google Adverts ads. Essentially, it is Google's assessment of your performance. You may raise your score by enhancing your keywords, ad copy, and user experience on your website.

Still, having issues? Can't decide what to do differently? Are your Google Ads ads simply not working?

All you need to do is... dial!

How to Contact Google Ads Support

Yes, Google has created a support service available to marketers, allowing anyone to set up their campaigns for free with the assistance of a professional, a true Google Ads Specialist.

Simply dial 800 694 113.

When it comes to improving your website's revenue and traffic, Google Ads is an exceptionally strong instrument.

However, this is not a magic formula; simply spending money on Google Ads will not ensure the success of your firm. On the contrary, as previously stated, it will take several attempts to select the ideal ad type for you.

But we are confident that with a little patience, you will be able to design fantastic campaigns for your business, whether you have a physical store or run your ecommerce using dropshipping.

CHAPTER 7

HOW GOOGLE ADS WORKS

It's likely that when you ran a Google search, you came across links that stuck out in the results. You've most likely visited a blog and noticed a banner ad somewhere on the page. Even when watching a YouTube video, some advertisements flashed before or during the video.

The three ad examples above are distinct: the first appears on a search engine, the second on a website, and the third on YouTube. They do, however, have one feature: they may all be launched or managed using Google Ads (AdWords) campaigns.

What exactly are Google Ads?

What are Google Ads? AdWords by Google

Google Ads, formerly known as Google Adwords, is the advertising platform and primary source of revenue for Google. Its initial version was released on October 23, 2000, and it has held the market leader position ever since.

Google AdWords profits were roughly $ 79 billion in 2016. The second spot is a little out of reach; consider Facebook advertising, which has a market capitalization of $26 billion.

AdWords income has increased dramatically since 2001, but what makes Google Ads such an intriguing advertising platform?

Companies can use this service to pay Google to promote their products or services on the Internet. But it's not quite that straightforward.

The most significant advantage of Google Ads is that ads may be shown to a highly targeted audience.

That is, it is not merely paying to appear more than once. You are investing in a qualified audience who is thus relevant to your business.

After all, is it more necessary for vegan food e-commerce to present your campaign to 10,000 individuals regardless of diet, or to 500 people who identify themselves as a vegan?

This is the fundamental principle of AdWords. Advertisers can control when their adverts display by using cookies and keywords.

Google Ads campaigns

With this platform you have the possibility to choose the type of Adwords campaign you want to develop:

Search network Display

Google Shopping

Video

Universal campaign for apps

Ads on the search network

These are the ads that appear in the search results for certain keywords. These will be positioned as featured results at the beginning and end of the SERP (Search Engine Results Page) and with a small notice saying "Ad", indicating that this is a sponsored link.

It is a particularly useful format for reaching people looking for specific products, services, or solutions. For the same reason, it is the most competitive type of campaign, as it allows you to display text ads directly in the most used search engine in the world for users who are looking for exactly what the company has to offer.

The big advantage here is that the advertiser only pays when the person clicks the result link to access the website. In other words, these ads can be very cost-effective for your business.

Ads on the Display Network

This campaign-style can be found on various websites, news pages, and blogs. They all make up the so-called Google Ads Display Network, which reaches 90% of Internet users worldwide.

In absolute numbers, Google's display ads appear on more than two million websites and in more than 650,000 applications.

Display ads have special targeting options: keywords, geographic information, and remarketing. With them, you can get customers to see your brand, consider your offers, and take action.

There are several ways to use display advertising:

Banner: these are graphic ads which can be images, interactive elements, animations, custom layouts, among others;

Text: it is similar to the banner but has a "text box" format, consisting of a title, a description, the company name, and a URL;

Gmail: These are personalized ads in Gmail that can be displayed directly in the user's inbox.

Apps: These are ads that appear specifically in mobile applications.

YouTube Ads

If you are a YouTube user, you must have already seen that some videos contain advertisements before starting or even during the video. Therefore, you can also create video-based campaigns on this platform.

With over a billion users, you can select the target audience you want based on age, gender, location, interest, and more.

Important detail: According to YouTube, you will only pay when people are interested in your campaign. That is, if the ad is skipped before 30 seconds (or before the end), you will not pay anything.

Ads by app

Here the ads are mainly focused on those who have applications and want to increase their reach with this Google platform. You can promote your business or even your application for iOS or Android users.

After a short setup, your ad will be qualified to reach over one million people on the Google Network, including Google

Search, Google Play, YouTube, as well as millions of websites and mobile apps.

Google Ads: How does it Work?

Well then does this all mean that I just have to pay and will magically appear to everyone in my market? Again, it's not that simple.

Google Ads works like an auction, meaning advertisers offer money in exchange for clicks. The advantage is that in AdWords the highest bid doesn't always win.

Google combines a few quality factors to evaluate ad position based on their Ad Rank. In short, it is not enough to give the best offer, it is important that the announcement is really good.

What is Google Ads Ad Rank made up of? In summary, Ad Rank is made up of:

$$P1 = (Q1 \times B2) / Q1$$

Q indicates quality B bidding, which is the maximum monetary value of the auction.

This means that even if your competitors' bids are higher than yours, your ad can stand out if your quality rating is higher.

How is the quality index calculated?

The quality index is an evaluation made by Google, which gives a score ranging from 1 to 10. This note, plus the bid, is what will determine the position of your ad for the keyword and the defined segmentation.

The components of the quality index are:

1. CTR;

2. Relevance;

3. Landing page.

How to create an account in Google AdWords (Ads)

Creating an account in Google Ads is very simple. To get started, go to the service page.

Click "Start Now". Then, write the Google email you want to link to your Ads account and your website.

By clicking "Continue", Google will run a setup wizard, providing you with all the details you need to create your ads account.

In the steps to follow, you will need to enter some data and set up a trial campaign (only if you wish) to start using ads.

How to create an ad in Google Ads?

So far we have talked about what AdWords is and how relevant it is on the internet today.

If you understand that Google Ads can be a great customer acquisition channel for your business, it's time to start creating ads:

The ad structure in Google Ads

The ad in Google AdWords is divided into four parts:

Final URL: This is the landing page the user will be directed to after clicking on the link. This address does not appear in the advertisement;

Title: it is the first line of the announcement, however its registration takes place in 2 lines of 30 characters, which will be separated by a hyphen in the title;

Path: a "fictional" but short address shown in green. Automatically includes the registered website in the final URL and allows for the inclusion of two sub-categories, with 15 characters each;

Description: the lines of text below, with a maximum size of 80 characters.

In the items below we will give you some tips on how to write each of these lines.

Tips for producing Google AdWords ads

The best way to be successful with your ad is to somehow tell whoever they are looking for that the ad is "made for them".

Placing the exact same search keyword in the title, for

example, tends to generate excellent results, mainly because the terms used by the user in the search, if present in the ad, are highlighted in bold and stand out.

Another option is to mention some specific features of the ad. Since in CPC mode you only pay Google for clicks this is to eliminate those clicks that your company is not interested in.

For example, someone who is not a student will likely not click on your ad if you clearly state "for students only".

Including pricing and payment methods also works as a filter and positively affects your ad's conversion rate.

When viewing an ad without price information, it is necessary to enter the website and evaluate this information, generating a click and, consequently, a collection.

Now, if the price is already in the ad, the price research phase has already moved into the search, making the potential visitor much more qualified and conversion-prone.

Some studies also show that capitalizing all words grabs attention and draws more clicks (Google itself recommends doing so).

There are also some specific suggestions for each part of the ad.

Assessment

The headline is the most striking part of the ad and should reflect what the user is looking for. If you don't have good ideas for the title of your Google Adwords ad, try some of our suggestions: Call the public by his name:

1. Management for freelancers

2. Accounting software

Go to the problem:

Internet problems?

Do you need a doctor?

 Be provocative:

Do you hate to wait? Tired of your TV?

Arouses curiosity:

The secret of the sale Are you a good boss?

Make a promise:

Sing better in 8 days End insomnia Provides information:

How to choose your mobile How to cook better

Description

As a matter of fact, you won't be able to put the entire sales presentation in just 80 characters. But remember that the goal here is just to attract the click. The other necessary information will be within your website.

In the descriptive lines it is interesting to highlight some topics that may arouse interest (or curiosity) and attract a click:

a)   A description of the resources and features: Solid wood furniture

2.0 engine, airbag, and leather seats

b)   A clear and concise benefit (or solution):

Save up to 15% energy Improve your teaching

c) A proposition that shows something in which you are different: Installation in just 1 day

10 years of experience

d)   A testimony or status indicator:

Featured in Magazine X Award Winner X

e)   A call:

Buy today Download

f) A phrase that alienates those who aren't your target audience: Only in Bogota

For multinationals

g)   A promotion:

Discounts of 40% Free trial for 10 days

View the URL

Due to the different and eye-catching color, that URL line is also very important. To choose the URL displayed, use the company's domain and try to summarize the offer you have for the user after the click.

For example, if I were offering an eBook, a good address would be: antoniodecarlo.it/eBook.

Destination URL

Another thing to choose is which page to direct people who click on your ad.

The best option is to direct the user to a page that has exactly what they are looking for and that has a perfect relationship with the ad.

A good landing page, created exclusively for the advertised offer, tends to generate much more results than a simple redirect to the homepage because it does not let the user discover for himself where the information is.

Google Ads ad extensions

In addition to the ad content itself, you can add ad extensions to include information that complements your offer and can also make a difference in the performance of your campaign.

Google is constantly updating ad extension types. For this reason, it is important to follow the official AdWords blog and also constantly evaluate the options of the tool itself. Currently, the available extensions are:

Sitelink: link to other pages of the website;

Phrase in the foreground: short phrases, where it is possible to highlight the differentials of the advertised product/service;

Structured Snippets: List of featured highlights such as brands, services, models, and courses;

Call: insertion of the phone in the announcement (on mobile devices it is possible to initiate the call directly via the announcement);

Message: allows the user to send a text message via their mobile phone, with content predetermined by the advertiser;

Local: allows you to include the company's address using the Google My Business account and view the user's distance;

Affiliate Local - Currently only available to auto dealers and retail networks in the US and UK;

Price: list of products, services, and even events, where you can include the price and specific links;

Applications: ad for Android or iOS applications;

Comments: Comments from customers and influencers (the comment must be registered on a page of the site); Automatic extensions: they are created automatically by Google when it expects that they can improve performance.

Extensions can be configured at the ad group level (displayed only alongside ads from the selected group), campaign (displayed with all ads in a campaign), and account (displayed on all active search ads in the account).

We recommend configuring ad groups to have extensions that are more relevant to your ad context.

Also when configuring the extensions you can determine the period in which they will be displayed (great for spreading promotions and events) and if they will only be displayed on mobile devices (interesting for developing exclusive extensions, such as a highlight phrase promoting the "free shipping by phone mobile phone ", for example).

Some extensions allow user clicks, such as sitelinks (which direct visitors to specific pages on your website), calls, and applications. If the user clicks on an extension and not the ad title, the cost-per-click value paid by the advertiser will be the same.

It is important to note that although all extensions are configured correctly, they will not always appear. Google will prioritize the extensions that are most relevant to the user and those that can generate the most results.

Dynamic ads

Dynamic Ads are a resource of advanced tools to ease the ad creation process and make your content more relevant. You can set up fully dynamic ads within AdWords or determine only a portion of your content.

Dynamic ad: When using a dynamic ad, you only need to include a description and a standard display URL. The title and the final URL are dynamically included by Google, taking into consideration the user's search and the relevance with the configured website;

Ad with dynamic attribute: configuration is done in a traditional text ad, where it is possible to configure an automatic countdown from a certain date, automatic insertion of the keyword that triggered the ad, or even an SE function, which can insert a certain text when a condition is met (navigation from a mobile device, for example). To include it, just open a brace "{" and you will see the options to configure them.

What not to do in ad copy: Google Ads policy

Google has an editorial policy and does not accept certain types of ads being displayed. So that your business can avoid falling into one of these mistakes, we reproduce here the main guidelines for texts in AdWords.

Spacing

There must be correct spacing between words and after punctuation. For example, "cheap clothes" are not allowed; "Free delivery. Buy" is not even.

Punctuation and symbols

Punctuation cannot be used to grab the user's attention. Also, the title cannot contain exclamation points, and the body of the ad can only contain one exclamation point in total.

All symbols, numbers, and letters must represent their true meaning (they must not be used in place of words). For example, "The best teachers" would violate this policy because

"The best teachers" would substitute for words.

Repetition of words

Word repetition should not be used as an advertising item or for promotional purposes. Likewise, the same word cannot be repeated three or more times on a line. For example, an ad with the headline "Business, business, business here" is not allowed.

To meet the requirements of these policies, the ad title must be replaced with a phrase such as "Incredible business here".

Improper language

Ads, including display URLs, may not contain language that is deemed inappropriate or offensive to some users. This also applies to misspellings, self-censorship, or other types of inappropriate language.

Unacceptable phrases

Some phrases may not appear in ad texts if they do not describe the product, service, or website. For example, a generic phrase like "click here" is not allowed. An example of a good phrase would be "Order online now", as it would represent the product and content of the site.

Use of the superlative

Superlatives are words that emphasize superiority. In order for users to feel treated honestly and reliably, the ad text cannot contain comparative or subjective phrases, such as

"The best" or "The number 1", unless the product or service is evaluated by associations of third parties.

This rating should be clearly visible on your website. For example, if your ad claims that a website is "Best on the Web," the site must show a third-party rating of that claim.

For example, a stamp from a specialist media stating that the company has received an award would be acceptable and the advertising would comply with Google AdWords policy.

In conclusion

Google Ads is a spectacular platform to use in sponsored link campaigns. For a complete digital marketing strategy, it is very important to consider this tool as a customer acquisition channel.

Now, you who are starting out, you have to keep in mind that this is a huge universe. You may make mistakes at first, but the important thing is that you can learn from them.

If the campaigns are well planned and executed correctly, you will later realize that this platform will be part of your strategy permanently.

CHAPTER 8

HOW TO SELL FOR FREE ON GOOGLE SHOPPING AND TAKE ADVANTAGE OF THIS SITUATION

Have you ever considered selling on Google Shopping? If you answered yes, you're in luck because Google stated on April 21st that it would give the ability to sell on Google Shopping for free.

This move will largely affect the United States, but Google intends to roll it out globally by the end of the year.

The search engine behemoth could not have chosen a better time for this announcement, as online store traffic has grown considerably as a result of the current pandemic. Google thinks that this will let "merchants connect more readily with consumers, regardless of whether they advertise on Google."

The option to use this sales channel for free could tip the scales for many small retailers who would otherwise be unable to afford to use Google's shopping channel.

Google allows you to boost the visibility of your store and show your products to the millions of individuals who use the platform every day.

How does Google Shopping operate, and what has changed?

Google Shopping ads, like Facebook or Instagram advertisements, are a great method to gain customers and increase sales to your online store. While drop shippers don't use Google Shopping advertisements as much as they do social media, they account for more than 16 percent of ecommerce site sales.

Google Shopping advertisements display at the top or right of the search results page (SERP). Of course, you may also find them on the Shopping tab. They differ from search results ads in that they incorporate product photos. Below, you may compare the Shopping results on the right, in the red box, to the regular search results.

Because Product Listing Advertisements (PLAs) provide customers with all of the necessary information - price, image, product name, and store name - those who see the ads have a better probability of making a purchase. Shopping, in fact, has a 30% greater conversion rate than text ads. Here are some of the factors that contribute to Google Shopping's success.

Previously, in order to have your products displayed on Shopping, you had to have accounts with both Google Merchant Center and Google Ads. Having a Merchant Center account allowed you to organize your product stream in a Google-compatible way, whilst Ads is where you could check offers and advertising.

Even with the new Google Shopping modifications, you will still require a Merchant Center account. This is due to the fact that in order to place your listing, you will still need to have all of your shop and product information in a Google compatible format. However, with Google Shopping for free, you do not need a Google Ads account to use the platform.

Google Shopping: the price. Are they required?

If you currently pay for Google Shopping advertisements, you may be wondering what this move implies for you. To begin, sure, paying for Google Shopping advertisements is still necessary.

While retailers will be able to market their products on Google Shopping for free, paying for advertisements will still have advantages. Paying for ads on Google Shopping, for example, will be the most effective strategy to secure the greatest positions for your products.

In addition, if you were previously just paying to have some of your products displayed, you may now post listings for all of your other products on Google Shopping for free. To accomplish this, ensure that all of your products are included in the Merchant Center product stream.

What is the best way to sell on Google Shopping?

As previously stated, even though Google Shopping is now free, you will not be able to receive adverts automatically.

To take advantage of this new possibility, you must first register your store with Google Merchant Center. If you are not currently a registered user, you must go through the registration process. The good news is that the Google Merchant Center support page contains a full onboarding guide that will coach you through the process.

Once you've enrolled in the Merchant Center, navigate to the "Growth" area and select "Manage programs."

It may appear to be a hard process, but if you utilize Shopify, there is an even faster way.

You may easily install the useful Google Shopping app by browsing the Shopify App Store. This software connects with Google Merchant Center and Google Ads, making it simple to add products.

After that, you'll need to enter your product feeds into your account to ensure your products appear. This method, like most Google products, is not only straightforward but also incredibly intuitive.

What if you sell outside of the United States?

You may have noticed that if you want to sell on Google but your target market is outside of the United States, you will have to wait a bit longer for this adjustment to take effect.

At the end of April, Google Shopping Ads became free in the United States. However, no specific date has been given for the international debut, however, the business has indicated that its goal is to "extend change globally before the end of the year."

Don't be discouraged if you're selling outside of the United States. Instead, utilize time to get everything back in order so that when the change goes into effect, you will be fully prepared and ready to go.

CHAPTER 9

GOOGLE MY BUSINESS: THE ULTIMATE GUIDE FOR YOUR BUSINESS

Online competition is becoming more severe in an almost entirely digital society. To develop their business, all entrepreneurs want to show higher in the SERP, and Google My Business is the key to doing so.

Consider this. If you want your brand to appear in the SERP for the keyword "furniture shop," you'll have to fight with giants like Ikea and Scavolini. Having a Google My Business listing, however, assists small and medium-sized businesses to rank higher in search results due to criteria such as keyword relevancy and customer reviews.

Google My Business brings enterprises of all sizes to the same level, allowing for the sharing of critical information that clients require in an easy-to-analyze style that enhances clicks and possibly conversion rate.

What exactly is Google My Business?

What exactly is Google My Business, and how does it function? Google My Business is a free tool that allows businesses to establish profiles that include key information about their operations, such as location, hours of operation, website links, and items or services supplied. This information is displayed in a section at the very top of the search results page.

Users can expand the list by clicking on this area, which will display additional businesses that match their search.

One issue that may be raised is, "How much does Google My Business cost?" You'll be surprised by the answer: nothing. Google My Business is a free service that allows you to build a profile for your business on the Google Search Network and

Google Maps in order to connect with customers.

Why should you utilize Google My Business?

Google My Business is a free service that provides a variety of benefits, the most notable of which is the increased visibility provided by the Google My Business card, which contains the most important information that your target audience needs.

Because most businesses do not claim their Google listing, you have the possibility to appear higher in the SERP results. If you are among the minority of people who not only claim the ad but also care about optimizing the profile, your chances of getting seen grow significantly.

Most users, for example, try to discover what purchase possibilities exist by searching on Google for the keyword "antique watches." As a result, Google My Business listings are more likely to reveal businesses that aren't exceptionally well-known or don't pay for sponsored listings.

GMB (Google My Business) displays reviews as well. If you have positive ratings, you will rank higher in the search results and will capture users' attention sooner, boosting the possibility of traffic to your site.

This platform also allows you to provide numerous ways for users to contact the advertisement, such as a phone number, a contact call to action that can be used to send text messages or a link with directions to the place in person.

Because most critical information (including frequently asked questions) is just a click away for consumers, the simplicity of accessing contact choices is an immensely effective tool that improves the possibility that they will choose to contact the business in the issue.

You may use the app to read, review, and manage all messages, as well as publish offers and respond to reviews if customers contact you using Google My Business. This makes interacting with your market segment exceedingly simple. You can get the app from iTunes or Google Play.

If the visibility and convenience of use for your consumers haven't yet convinced you, bear in mind that Google also provides analytics tools to help you keep track of everything linked to your profile. You'll have data to understand how many people are watching and interacting with your profile this way, and you'll be able to evaluate your progress and track the efficacy of your adjustments.

How to Add Your Company to Google

The procedure of registering your business on Google My Business is fairly straightforward.

Begin by entering your company name here.

After you enter your company name, Google will ask you to select the category that best represents your company.

If your company has a physical location, you must include the address and display the Google indicator on the map so that clients can quickly find you.

Google My Business will also inquire if you offer your services outside of this location, such as if you make deliveries or give home services.

Google Maps for Business

If you own an ecommerce site, make Google aware of this option and include the territories serviced by your services. By doing so, you will boost your chances of appearing in relevant searches for your market.

Finally, in order to begin maintaining your profile, you must provide your contact information and complete the creation of your Google My Business listing.

How to Authenticate Your Google My Business Listing

Google will prompt you to authenticate your business and confirm that you own it once you've created your Google My Business listing. In this manner, you can manage your company's information on Google, ensuring that it appears first in searches and on geo-localized maps.

Immediately after creating your Google My Business listing, you will be prompted to select a method of verification. The verification procedure is simple and quick.

Verification by post: You will receive a postcard with a code that you can use for online confirmation.

Verify by phone: Google will call the provided business number and give you a code for online confirmation.

Verification by email: available only for a certain business category, it allows you to receive the verification code to a company email address.

Businesses that have previously registered their website with the search engine can check their listings immediately, however, this option is not available for all industries.

How to Improve Your GMB Board

After you finish your Google My Business verification, you will have complete control over your listing, allowing you to properly optimize it. The goal of optimization will be to provide users with enough information to entice them to click while also ensuring that you take the required steps to go up the SERP results.

Let's look at four crucial stages to discover how to make the most of Google My Business.

1 . Fill out your profile

Many local businesses only fill out the minimum information provided during the registration process and never go out of their way to fill out their profile.

This is a blunder that must be avoided at all costs.

Your goal is to create a profile that is as complete as possible. This will bring value to those who visit your profile because they will immediately grasp what your company offers and how to contact you. It also allows you to insert relevant keywords in the description, which will help you appear in more searches and improve your visibility.

Your listing should ideally include the following information:

A description of your company and basic information about the products and services you provide.

Information on your distinctive sales argument, which can help you differentiate your company from the competition.

Photographs of your goods, services, or locations.

Contact information, address, and hours of operation

Responses to any questions posed by your audience.

2. Get reviews

Reviews are crucial since Google's algorithm is designed to make businesses with a higher number of good reviews more accessible to searchers. Furthermore, having reviews will drive potential buyers to your listing and help them trust you sooner.

Up to 88 percent of consumers believe internet reviews as much as they do a personal recommendation, and 72 percent are more ready to trust a firm after reading a positive review. Given that 92 percent of consumers read online reviews before making a purchase, having a large number of reviews with an average rating of 4 or 5 stars will have an impact on your Google My Business profile.

As a result, attempting to obtain Google My Business evaluations in an ethical but planned manner should be an important element of your marketing strategy. Contact your clients a few weeks after they've made a purchase to ensure they're satisfied and to ask them if they'd be willing to help your business develop by providing a review. On Shopify, there are various tools that can assist you to handle the request for reviews in order to maximize the likelihood of positive responses from users.

Make an effort to respond to your customers' evaluations as they come in. According to Google, businesses that reply to reviews are 1.7 times more trustworthy than those that do not. Take a few moments to thank people who left you a positive review and respond to any comments by offering to remedy the issue in private.

3. Employ several keywords

Having a major keyword in mind while you create your business description is a wonderful idea, but it doesn't mean you have to stick to just one.

Understand the terms that people use to find businesses like yours, and make sure you enter the most relevant keywords with the highest search volume. Only be wary about employing too many keywords!

In most circumstances, including location-based keywords can help you enhance local search presence without limiting your business's reach.

4. Select a specialty category

When you establish your Google My Business listing, you must select a category that best describes your business. Some categories are more general, such as "jewelry", and "jeweler". Others, on the other hand, are decidedly more specific, such as "jewelry engraver", and "jewelry repair service".

When choosing the category for your business, make sure you are as specific as possible. If you were to choose too large a category, you will collide with a higher number of competitors and you may not be able to get in touch with potential customers who are looking for the product or service that your business offers.

Google My Business is a powerful tool that gives brands the opportunity to get noticed by customers. If you've ever wondered if you should take advantage of Google My Business listings, stop thinking about it and sign up. It takes very little time to sign up, verify your business and optimize it for success, and you'll be one step closer to connecting with more people in your target market.

CHAPTER 10

WHAT ARE CONTENT MARKETING, EXAMPLES, AND STRATEGIES?

Why should you use a content marketing strategy? Because, despite the fact that there is a lot of content of all kinds available, it still functions excellently!

Content marketing can still be a business's secret weapon. Updating your blog on a regular basis, releasing new vlogs, podcasts, or discussing your business on social media will greatly assist you in attracting new consumers!

What exactly is content marketing?

If you've never heard of content marketing, you might find it difficult to understand. Content marketing entails creating content relating to your company or brand; this might include blog entries, videos, podcasts, social media postings, ebooks, infographics, and other forms of media.

The goal is to employ content generation to enhance traffic and thus profit.

It is critical to remember that your content must be of good quality and deliver relevant information to your customers. If the content is utilized to spread false information or to draw new people closer to your brand, you will almost certainly have the opposite effect. Poor and irrelevant material does not pique the interest of users, who will notice and rarely buy from your store, and you will have squandered important time.

Social media marketing and content marketing

When it comes to content marketing, the blog is frequently the first thing that comes to mind. Create your own space where you can share useful information about your brand and the market sector into which you have entered by writing articles.

As a result, let's begin by examining the relationship between content marketing and social media: let's flip the traditional sequence to shake up your approach to digital communication!

Let us begin with an important clarification:

Content marketing and social media marketing are two distinct entities with distinct dynamics.

Consider this: In the first example, you would go to create material focused on your target audience; in the second, you would not only be talking to your audience, but you would also be addressing that segment (more or less small) that is on that social network. To put it mathematically, you are speaking to a subset of the intended audience!

Another significant distinction is that with content marketing, you can choose from the various forms of content available, however on social media, you are limited by the platform: you will not be able to publish a long post on Instagram, just as you will not be able to publish a narrative on Pinterest.

As a result, content marketing must be woven into the platform like an haute couture gown. The following is a shortlist of the most engaging content, organized by social media:

Facebook: instructions, product photos, videos (with subtitles because many people do not turn on the music), content that tells stories, inspirational postings, sharing of blog articles and materials;

Instagram: interactive stories (questions, quizzes, votes, polls...), user-contributed content, profile shoutouts, inspiring posts, giveaways, and contests;

Linkedin: graphs, infographics, job ads, job search, case studies, viral examples, motivational posts, blog posts, webinars, premium materials, and questions

TikTok: a challenge, a lesson, an instructive film, branded filters, a prize, and a contest;

YouTube tutorials, vlogs, reviews, live events, reactions, and experiments

Twitter: breaking news and updates, polls, gifs, memes, announcements, teaser trailers, and product launches.

Content Marketing vs. SEO

SEO and content marketing complement one other and are sometimes used interchangeably. Is it possible to have content without SEO? Yes. Can SEO exist in the absence of content? In this case, the answer is less immediate, but it is, in a sense, yes (an example is a technical SEO and the use of Schema markup).

Let's compare them to Doctor Frankenstein and Igor: they're great on their own, but they're even better when they're together!

If it's evident that SEO can be less effective for social media content, you're undoubtedly wondering, "but sorry, don't all blog articles have to be optimized for search engines?" That's an excellent question.

The truth is that not every content is designed to rank high indefinitely: consider the news: no one will look at online purchasing statistics from four years ago; everyone wants the most up-to-date information! The same may be said for product updates. They are service articles with little or no relation to SEO.

But what if I wanted to optimize an article to rank top on a search engine result page? Here are some brief pointers to consider:

Use an SEO tool to find keywords with medium-high search volumes (500-1000 searches per month) but low difficulty (calculated on a scale of 0 to 100, with 0 indicating terms that are relatively easy to enter and 100 indicating impossible queries).

Ensure that your content matches the search intent of your users! You risk not attracting clicks;

Consider the lineup with the goal of providing the most full and attractive content on that topic ever;

Begin writing by entering your main keyword a few times (don't overdo it, though, because you risk keyword stuffing).

Complete your content by introducing internal and external links.

Content marketing vs. inbound marketing

We conclude our comparison assessment by asking if content marketing and inbound marketing are the same things. And, once more, the answer is no.

Inbound marketing is a far bigger field than content marketing: it encompasses email marketing, web design, advertising, and so on... creating content is merely one component of the inbound approach.

In truth, there is inbound content, but there is also

outbound content, such as chilly commercials, and invasive pop-ups with a cross to shut them that cannot be detected unless you have an eagle eye on the hunt... Between the two tactics, there is an overlap - again, thanks to math - but that doesn't mean they are the same.

What are the primary advantages of content marketing for a company's internet presence?

Increased brand awareness

You may raise brand recognition by disseminating material on a broad scale and through different communication channels. Consider an infographic: imagine making one and publishing it on LinkedIn.

This form of material has a high viral load since it displays data and statistics that can be valuable to a larger number of individuals. Consider all of the people who will click "Recommend": your material will move from profile to profile, emphasizing the brand that developed it.

When deciding who to buy from or partner with, the consumer will go with the company "he's already heard of."

Site traffic has increased (even at no cost)

The main advantage of content marketing is that it drives traffic to your website. We can intercept a new audience that does not yet know us with SEO and sponsored posts, and we can care for and discourse with the audience we have already obtained through social media posts.

Obviously, SEO takes longer to bear fruit, but if you get

into the appropriate gear, you may get traffic for free, even from very old posts!

Assistance to the sales and customer service teams

Remember when we discussed service material that wasn't explicitly focused on SEO positioning? We're about to show you how valuable it is!

Consider how frequently your sales and customer service staff are asked the same questions. Don't you think it's a waste of time that could be avoided? Create a FAQ area, write articles to solve the most common problems... in a word, improve your customer service!

This information will assist you in optimizing the internal resources at your disposal and increasing the productivity of your team!

How to Develop a Successful Content Marketing Strategy

We discussed content marketing in all of its forms, tried to differentiate it from other methods, and showed why to use it and the major benefits for your organization... but now we need substance! So, here's a step-by-step guide to developing a winning content marketing strategy.

1. Determine your objectives.

What is your content marketing campaign's goal? Whether it's earning X number of followers, increasing organic traffic to the site, or attaining a particular number of subscribers, little changes: what matters is that we create a goal that will serve as a beacon in the dark and guide us in the correct direction.

How do you set a goal? Consider using the SMART technique. It is an English abbreviation for:

Specific: select a specific, measurable goal... As our second argument illustrates, a target that is overly broad risks not being easily measured.

Measurable: How do you know whether you've met a goal like "grow Instagram followers"? It is virtually impossible. If, on the other hand, you had set a target like "grow Instagram followers by 20%," you would know if you succeeded or not at the end of the campaign.

Achievable: It's fine to aim high and be ambitious, but we also need to keep grounded. If you've just established a blog, setting a goal of 100k organic visits in a month may be impossible, and you'll wind up giving up for no reason. If you now have a 10% growth rate, attempt to establish a 15% growth rate for yourself!

Relevant: What advantages would you get if you achieved this? When deciding on a target, keep the cost/benefit ratio in mind.

Time-based (With a deadline): Set a deadline for yourself, such as reaching 1000 followers within three months of launching my Instagram page. This will allow you to insert intermediate checkpoints, such as "Am I on the correct track?" What aspects of my goal-achievement strategy might I improve?

2. Determine the target audience

To whom am I speaking? Of course, to the intended

audience. But who are these individuals? What are their hobbies? What kinds of content do they like? What channels do they use to obtain information? What are his difficulties, and how can I assist him in overcoming them?

These and other questions must be addressed while determining your target audience.

We're talking about buyer personas, which are a fairly simple approach to creating an identikit of your typical reader. They are fictitious representations of your ideal consumer that allow you to simply identify the topics to discuss and the channels you must not miss.

Start by conducting market research, interviewing consumers or potential customers, and conducting research on social networks such as Facebook or LinkedIn.

3. Ciak! Act!

Once the goal has been determined and the audience has been identified, all that remains is to take the stage!

If you've done your target research correctly, you should have a good idea of which channels to include in your content marketing strategy.

When you're going to start typing, keep in mind that you're not writing for yourself, but for anybody you want to read to you.

So, avoid strange literary techniques, strive to be open and honest if your purpose is to inform, entertaining if you want to entertain, and professional at all times.

However, as previously said, the content includes not only text but also pictures. Complement your postings with eye-catching photographs that are consistent with your brand image - this is an indirect method to build your brand identity.

Even in the field of design, even the most inexperienced can find ways to post content that has a professional appearance and feel: Canva is unquestionably the must-have tool in this situation. It is great for people looking for a DIY solution that may provide a visually pleasing output, thanks to its templates (both free and paid) and library of images and icons.

Keep in mind that each platform has its unique measurements!

Remember to always verify the ratio of the postings if you don't want your faces to be chopped off from the image (on Canva you often have templates with the correct formats already preset).

This is especially true on social media! Within the same platform, there is a square image with a 1: 1 ratio and a tale with a 16: 9 ratio and the risk of becoming confused is only around the corner that peeks out.

4. Evaluation of the findings

There are several KPIs to monitor depending on the sort of material and the goal you want to achieve to determine if you are on the correct track. Here are some KPIs to consider while developing organic content marketing strategies:

Organic visits: how many visitors come to your site from

a search engine result page?

Keyword Positioning: How has your position improved?

New and recurring visitors: Can you attract new users while retaining your current visitor base?

Backlinks: How many sites have linked to your material because they thought it was interesting?

Likes, comments, and shares are indicators of user engagement.

Let's now look at the analytics for paid content marketing strategies:

CPA (Expense Per Acquisition): the cost of achieving a conversion;

CPC (Cost Per Click);

Quality score: an important metric to monitor to ensure that the ad is relevant to those who find it.

Obviously, these are only instances, but the list could go on and on!

Best practices for content marketing

Are you looking for the greatest keywords? Done. Topics that are of interest to your target audience should be published. This has also been done. So, what are the best techniques for content marketing? Here are a few hints!

Content repurposing

When you think of content marketing, the first thing that comes to mind is deciding what topic to write about in a new blog post. Too frequently, we forget that not all of the stuff we create has to remain completely unpublished!

The optimal way to maximize your production is to re-propose information in many forms: from a video or podcast, you can obtain a transcript and use it as material for an article, or you may extrapolate micro-pills to replicate as stories, reels, or TikTok.

We all understand the value and importance of recycling, so why not apply it to content marketing as well?

Allow your audience to create.

We are so immersed in our market niche that, after a while, unique ideas run out and we fall back on tired and overused clichés. This is due to the fact that we forget we have an audience!

For any type of business, user-contributed material is creative lymph.

Ask your followers to submit content ideas in the comments, start a conversation, and reblog all the individuals who tag you in their photos on your channels... Often, all that is required to fill the editorial calendar is to simply listen.

Customize your content

In marketing, there is no such thing as a one-size-fits-all solution in theory or practice... or even in content. And the more posts there are on the market, the more we have to try to stand out: how? With tailored content.

In this regard, the message of Vidyard, an American firm specializing in video marketing, is intriguing. I've received their letters multiple times, and to my amazement, the welcome email included a video with my name on the cover! I had no doubts: the message was tailor-made for me.

Having individualized communication is a technique to put the user at the center of your thoughts and demonstrate how important he is to your company. It's a fantastic method to broaden your audience.

Worst practices: the most typical content marketing blunders

So, now that we've covered what to do, let's look at what to avoid if you want to establish an effective content marketing strategy.

Content should be written in stone.

You've created the best SEO post in the world, the ultimate advice, and the ideal content. You're pleased with your effort, aren't you? The biggest error you might do is to leave it on your site for months, if not years.

The world is continuously evolving, and the information you generate must reflect this. So, instead of writing articles in stone, let us create them on river water: a continuous flow in which we go to update the contents we make in order to keep them always current and genuine.

Develop a single-channel strategy.

You've been working on your blog for months, and you've worked hard to get your content to the first page... Then Google tweaks the algorithm, and your traffic mysteriously vanishes overnight.

Developing a single-channel approach is like jumping out of a plane without a backup parachute: what do you do if the first one fails to open?

The good news is that it is simple to correct: just diversify traffic by incorporating outlets relevant to your target demographic into your content marketing strategy. Create a company profile on all social networks gradually: the risk is that you won't be able to keep up!

Instead, strive to constantly post material on a few channels, and establish a fresh follower base from other traffic sources. It will come in handy, as you will see!

Examples of content marketing

Marketing through content

Chiara Ferragni, a prominent Italian digital entrepreneur, founded her blog The Blonde Salad in 2009; for some years now, it has been a very popular brand, and its store sells clothing, shoes, and accessories. The site's blog, on the other hand, is not attempting to entice new clients. It focuses on offering entertaining and highly relevant material to its target audience. Some articles may mention products from the line, but they will never blatantly try to sell them to you. This is also an excellent example of social sharing: the brand's Instagram profile currently has over 1 million followers.

The Blonde Salad is a blog for people who work from home.

Erbolario, a brand of natural body care products, is another example of a brand that uses a blog to deliver unique material to its visitors. Most major firms have ecommerce in addition to physical storefronts, and the most observant pay special attention to the blog. The contents offered here, too, do not simply market the brand's products, but also share important ideas and information that their target audience will undoubtedly find interesting!

In addition to selling its products, Royal Canin has made its website a very entertaining and useful resource. Their target audience is clear: pet owners and the numerous articles accessible provide information that is completely pertinent to this audience. It is not necessary for readers to purchase their items, though they may do so if they so desire: their purpose is to get their brand known and to position themselves as a reference platform in this industry.

Content marketing is an excellent approach to improving traffic, brand awareness, and sales. Creating quality content is critical if you want your store to be successful in the long run. Creating material on a regular basis can be exhausting, but don't let that deter you - there are numerous tools available to help you out. Remember to be patient; a few blog entries will not get you to the top of the search results. The wait may be long, but the results will be well worth it. When done correctly, content marketing will secure your store's success!

CHAPTER 11

B2B CUSTOMERS

Strategies for finding them

Finding B2B customers may not seem easy. The first tool that comes to mind is LinkedIn, of course, but it's not the only option. There are many other ways that the web offers, suitable for finding business customers regardless of the sector in which one operates. The important thing is to know them and to know how to exploit them.

The first thing to know is that not all acquisition methods are the same. There are tools capable of bringing few potential customers, but are highly qualified, others that bring many but are of low quality. This is why we need to compare the advantages to the disadvantages and find the right mix between volume, quality, budget, and time.

Cold calling

Used by many companies, cold calling is a commercial technique that consists of contacting professionals/companies by telephone that have no relationship with the company. A technique which - although now outdated, as it requires the training of sales-oriented and relationship-oriented operators - continues to be used above all by less digital companies.

Cold-emails

Among the methods most used by companies to find business customers are cold e-mails, the 2.0 version of cold calling. Obviously, e-mails must be written with criteria: they must go straight to the point, explain to the recipient why that product/service can improve their work, and tell who you are and what the values of your company are.

Trade fairs

In a digital world, attending a trade show can be seen as a bit of an old way to find new customers. In reality, this is not the case. Even today, fairs help to increase one's visibility and customer base, especially if one operates in "technical" sectors. However, they require a major investment, and - above all - they need to be planned in the best possible way.

There are several ways to participate in a trade show:

• you can have your own stand

• you can be invited as a speaker (the best solution, because it offers great visibility and does not require a financial outlay)

• you can sponsor the event

• you can visit the stands which you propose

Content marketing

To bring customers to you, to lead them on your site and therefore on your e-commerce (or on your contact form), content marketing is essential. You need to have a nice site that is responsive and has quality photographs. But, above all, you have to take care of its contents according to a very specific strategy. Some idea?

Start a blog and post at least two pieces of content per week

Publishes e-books and case studies

Post your articles on LinkedIn

Create YouTube videos

Be active on the forums

Online advertising

Advertising is a great way to find new B2B customers, but it does require some investment. The best platforms to bet on are:

Google Adwords

Facebook Ads

Ads on Linkedin and Twitter

It is essential to have the assistance of a professional who knows how to create campaigns in the right format and build them to reach an audience that is actually interesting. Especially in B2B, knowing where to hit is essential: professionals are short on time and don't click on ads that leave them dubious. On the contrary, they must be convinced that that product/service is really useful for their work.

Collaborations

Collaborations with other companies and other professionals allow you to exchange visibility at no cost. For partnerships to be successful, however, you need to select partners who have the same target customer like you but are not in direct competition with you. How do concretize the collaborations? Exchanging blog posts, inserting an advertisement for your company in the newsletter of the other (and vice versa), organizing webinars and common events, dividing the booth of a fair.

Offline marketing

Don't overlook the power of offline marketing. It is true that today, a lot is played on the web. However, traditional marketing continues to play a role in B2B. Depending on what your business is, it can be useful to make flyers (as long as they are eye-catching!) And distribute them in the mail or in a crowded place (like the subway exit). But you can also make commercials for radio and TV, if your budget allows it, or think of posters or guerrilla marketing actions that turn the spotlight on your company.

CHAPTER 12

SET THE STANDARD IN DIGITAL MARKETING

Lead generation is one of the most sought-after objectives for marketers wanting to convert and enhance their earnings. To begin, do you understand what a lead is or what it implies in the context of marketing? You may be aware, that such leads do not result in clients.

What exactly is a lead in the context of web marketing?

A lead is a user who has provided information to a corporation and so becomes a user with whom the company can communicate. This registration can be completed in person, using pen and paper, or online, using a contact form.

In this step, there is a critical transaction in which the user exchanges personal data with the company in exchange for something, such as access to specialized content, a data sheet, a product catalog for other companies, and so on.

However, before proceeding, keep in mind that there are various methods to comprehend what a lead, contact, or registration is, depending on the stage of the marketing campaign, the user's purchase process, or the level of engagement with the business. That is why, even in the realm of online marketing, there is often some misunderstanding when it comes to leads.

For its part, the corporation can reach the user nearly as if it were a two-way communication, but in a non-intrusive and practically undetectable manner. How do you go about it? This procedure will be done by automated marketing approaches so that the company may connect with this user and then send him communications, share content that may be of interest to him for the phase of the buying cycle in which he is placed, and also make commercial offers.

The main notion is that, as a result of the conversion into a lead, we will be able to contact this individual, who is no longer a faceless stranger, and provide him content connected to our product or service.

To treat a user as a lead, the user must have agreed to the company's privacy policies. This authorization is even more crucial now that the new European GDPR regulation has been implemented to govern the processing of personal data and the proper usage of cookies.

Lead science is not an exact science: a lead will have varying definitions depending on the industry and aims of each organization, as well as where the user is in the marketing funnel.

How do you get a lead?

A lead can be generated by any offline channel, such as physical forms, at an event, at a trade fair, to enter a raffle or receive a discount in-store, over the phone, and so on.

The majority of leads in a normal business marketing project are generated online. That is why, in this chapter, we will concentrate on leads generated via the internet channel, which may be collected in a variety of methods (organic search, social networks, direct traffic, etc.) and in a thousand different ways, depending on the actions we do and our social strategy.

In marketing, how does this happen?

Users typically notice fascinating stuff, desire to download it and fill up a form with their information. It is critical to provide valuable content via a form designed expressly to boost conversion. This can be found on a landing page, webpage, blog post, Facebook Lead format ad campaign, and so on.

As a result, in order to begin producing leads for your organization, you must first generate intriguing and high-quality content for your target audience and make it available for distribution via several modules.

Why are leads crucial to a business?

As you are aware, a lead is a person who is interested in your organization and may become a customer, even if they are not currently interested in our products or services. This is why leads are at the heart of any online marketing plan.

A technique in which we must gradually persuade our users that our products or services are of interest to them and successful in addressing their worries or requirements. Relax, your turn will come. Almost all of these techniques are targeted at acquiring clients, but you have to travel a long distance to do it.

How to Get More Leads

To accomplish this, we must attract traffic to our content via unique deals or promotions. This is known as "Lead Magnet."

We will need to provide an incentive as an enticement for users. For example, our prospective users can leave their information in exchange for a downloaded pdf of their choice, admission to a course, and so on. If they do this action and give their contact information, they will be qualified leads.

If this does not occur, it is possible that you have contacted folks who are completely outside your ideal target audience.

Most of the people who are about to contact us are in the early phases of the purchasing process, so we aren't interested in attracting only those who want to acquire the product or service. Our objective is to reach those who do not yet realize they require our product and to walk them through the entire process.

We achieve this, as I like to say, by giving the appropriate content at the right moment.

However, if we only generate visitors, the individual reads the information, and then leaves the website, we are not making a long-term influence. As a result, we must transform these anonymous visits into leads (not all of them convert, only a percent which can be around 1-5 percent).

So we may continue the conversation and stay in touch with them.

Getting an advantage is a critical point at which a person transitions from being anonymous on our website to knowing a little more about who they are, where to contact them, what requirements they may have, and how we can best support them with your content, goods, services, training, and so on.

Creating a database of these leads is critical in online marketing.

It is one of the most important assets for carrying out the strategy's most involved phases: lead nurturing and lead scoring.

Issues with lead quality in marketing and sales

When there are continual complaints or "disagreements" over lead quality, the biggest conflict between marketing and sales occurs. While digital marketers are proud of the enormous number of leads they have created, the sales department is irritated by the repeated rejection of prospects who were eventually uninterested.

This is how what appeared to be potential customers turned into low-quality leads; thus, the marketing department bears responsibility.

What different kinds of leads are there?

To begin, we must understand the following distinction: Hot leads vs. cold leads

What we've seen is the marketing definition of a lead: a person who may be interested in the firm. So much so that when a person is classified as a lead, they can be assigned to one of several groups based on:

- Resemblance to our buyer persona (ideal client).

- The stage of the purchasing process at which it is found.

- His involvement with the brand.

So the lead is interested in your industry, he could be a customer, he could not be ready yet, or he could be. However, if you ask a sales department, they will tell you that a lead is a possible customer, someone who is genuinely interested in what we have to offer.

In theory, a person who downloads content is a cold lead who is not ready to buy. It is a person who initiates a study or learning process in order to find a solution to a need or problem.

After the cold leads, we have the hot leads, which are folks who have already done some study and have a better idea of how to address their problem. Perhaps they are weighing the benefits and drawbacks of several alternatives, as well as their budget, forum reading, or research into how that service or product has worked for others. Finally, when it comes to leads, we aim for what is known as a "hot lead": people who are ready and willing to buy our product or service.

With this in mind, there is a great deal of ambiguity: Is every lead a sales opportunity?

143

No, just the contrary. In some businesses, a lead is someone who wants business information and has left information because they are interested in something. You could be interested in our content but not in the products we sell. Nothing happens, and everything is perfectly normal.

Differentiate leads in the purchasing process.

Continuing with the categories of leads, we find distinct leads depending on their stage and maturity level, distinguishing the following terms:

• Lead: a person who filled out a form to download information, sign up for a webinar, and so on. He has submitted your basic information (at least your email address) and acknowledged the legal notice in this form. It's still a long way away from the final deal, so it's a cold lead.

• A Marketing Qualified Lead, or MQL, is generated by marketing, typically automatically via lead nurturing and lead scoring. He has already expressed interest in the company's content on multiple occasions, indicating that he is at a more advanced stage of the purchasing cycle and is adapting to the buyer persona.

• An SQL, or Sales Qualified Lead (in English, 'Sales Qualified Lead'), is a leader who has reached the most advanced level of the buying process and is thus ready to buy. They are people who are generally moving up the marketing funnel and reacting to an offer that is much closer to the company's product or service (for example, a demonstration, a trial of the service, a commercial phone call...).

What are the key distinctions between MQL and SQL?

To comprehend the difference between a qualified lead for marketing and one qualified for sales, you must first understand that there may be multiple levels between the two.

Not everything will be determined by our industry, but also by the type of user, as it might be a leader who, in our opinion, is not ready for sale (and the seller will not be able to make him lose interest). This is why, using the lead scoring technique described below, you must determine which group the user belongs to.

To determine whether a prospect is MQL or SQL, we may look at the following categories.

• Leads who are uninterested and unsuitable for your company: These are people who are researching their competitors or, for other reasons, present incorrect data and have no interest in what you have to offer.

• Lead is very interested but insufficient: although showing interest in your material, it does not meet the qualities of your buyer persona. For example, we know she is a minor with insufficient purchasing power.

• Lead suitable for your firm, but less interested: it requires maturation, and we must continue to accompany it through the purchase process.

• Lead who is a good fit for your firm and is eager to learn SQL!

On the other hand, we must consider an earlier phase, that of the members.

Is a lead the same as a subscription to a newsletter?

We must not mix leads with subscribers, or, more specifically, we must not confuse lead nurturing with delivering the newsletter that includes our weekly offer.

A user at an early stage of the purchase cycle is typically referred to as a lead, but there is an earlier stage that should not be overlooked: subscribers.

Subscribers are users who have expressed an interest in our firm and have requested that we keep in touch with them, have subscribed to a newsletter, or have subscribed to a blog. While they simply provide us with their email (or other contact information) for this purpose, downloadable content may be offered indirectly in order to convert leads.

Is it true that a newsletter subscriber is less interested than a lead?

The answer is yes, albeit the majority of leads come from people who locate one of our pieces of material on the internet, download it, and then vanish into thin air. A subscriber, on the other hand, wants to receive information from us on a regular basis, which we should not underestimate.

You might believe that in an ideal plan, all of the leads we receive should be qualified. However, it is unavoidable that people will come to us who do not fit our customer persona and will not purchase. It is impossible to prevent obtaining unskilled leads.

Capturing leads who do not fit our buyer persona, on the other hand, is beneficial to us. We can build a community of people who read everything we publish and follow us on social media. They assist us in disseminating the material, sharing it, like us on social media, reading our emails, and so on.

How do lead generation strategies work?

To get quality leads, I manually write valuable content and provide it on a landing page. To access it, the user needs to complete a form, leave their information and become a lead. This is the traditional method, although there are other options for obtaining leads. For example, using a chatbot, social login, content updates, and so on.

Because the consumer is conducting research and discovery, the information we provide must be of high value and connected with the purchasing process to the point where the user is prepared to leave their data with the organization.

The promise of value must be met through the quality of the material; otherwise, we will collect data but develop mistrust, and this individual will not want to learn more about us.

You must undertake traffic attraction actions to get people to this content.

Users arrive at the landing page via a CTA (call to action), which we position in high traffic and visibility places of the site. It is usually through the blog (by providing a lot of material, we can obtain a lot of traffic), but it may also be through emails, social media, online adverts, and so on...

What are the possibilities for leads?

We assist the customer throughout the purchasing process. As you can see from the beginning, this is possible with lead nurturing and lead scoring.

Let's take a closer look at how it works:

1. Lead nurturing: As you will see throughout the text, the purpose of lead nurturing is to "mature" the leads, that is, to move them through the purchasing process until the final transaction. We normally do this through automatic contact with the person, such as automated email chains. However, you may also

Keep in touch through customized site content, retargeting efforts, and so forth. The idea is to deliver the relevant content at the right moment to "educate" or show the customer how to solve his problem, while also promoting ourselves as reference points and industry experts.

2. Lead scoring: Using this strategy, you will be able to categorize leads based on the buyer persona with which they align, their needs, behavior, and the stage of the buying process in which they are. In other words, this technique automatically provides a numerical score to each lead in a database based on the features and actions taken in relation to the company and its contents using a set of pre-established guidelines. Obviously, knowing all of this information with 100 percent confidence is difficult, but we can get a decent

estimate. The higher the score, the more you resemble the buyer persona, the more you interact with the page, and the more the material is purchase-driven.

A company can more simply implement specific actions for each of the groups if leads are ranked based on their score. It's also great for seeing business prospects and determining which leads are ready to convert and which aren't.

In order to produce results, an effective marketing plan necessitates the acquisition of leads. Otherwise, we will create content and attract people while accomplishing nothing.

We want to keep in touch with these folks since that is how we will be able to cultivate these relationships and identify sales prospects. As a result, we will gather their contact information and enter it into our database using very valuable material. We will "warm-up" these contacts in this way, through lead nurturing and lead scoring so that some will not be ready to buy.

www.ingramcontent.com/pod-product-compliance
Lightning Source LLC
LaVergne TN
LVHW020607200726
843509LV00001B/13